D1262994

THE PROBLEM OF THE SELF
IN BUDDHISM AND CHRISTIANITY

THE PROBLEM
OF THE SELF
IN BUDDHISM
AND CHRISTIANITY

Lynn A. de Silva

Foreword by
John Hick

BARNES & NOBLE
BOOKS
10 East 53d St., New York 10022
(a division of Harper & Row Publishers, Inc.)

BQ
4262
.D47
1979

291.22 D45

De Silva, Lynn A.

The problem of the
self in Buddhism and
Christianity

Foreword © John Hick 1979

Text © Lynn A de Silva 1975, 1979

All rights reserved. No part of this publication may be
reproduced or transmitted, in any form or by any means,
without permission

First published in a limited edition by The Study Centre
for Religion and Society, Colombo, Sri Lanka, 1975

This edition first published 1979 by
THE MACMILLAN PRESS LTD
London and Basingstoke

Published in the U.S.A. 1979 by
HARPER & ROW PUBLISHERS, INC.
BARNES & NOBLE IMPORT DIVISION

Printed in Great Britain

Library of Congress Cataloging in Publication Data

De Silva, Lynn A   1919–
   The problem of the self in Buddhism and Christianity.

   Library of philosophy and religion)
   Includes indexes.
   1. Anātman. 2. Man (Theology). 3. Christianity
and other religions – Buddhism. 4. Buddhism – Relations
– Christianity. I. Title.
BQ4262.D47   1978   291.2'2   76–19860

ISBN   0–06–491667–7

DABNEY LANCASTER LIBRARY
LONGWOOD COLLEGE
FARMVILLE, VIRGINIA 23901

Contents

79— 2659

Foreword

For many centuries the great world religions developed as separate and more or less self-contained streams of life, wrapped in mutual ignorance. The occasional contacts between them were mostly hostile, and often violent, and permitted very little in the way of constructive dialogue. However, during the last hundred years or so our knowledge of mankind's religious life has been accumulating and indeed multiplying through the labours of scholars, and as a result the world religions have become conscious of one another in a new way. Within the last few decades inter-religious dialogue has begun in many parts of the world. This is bound to influence the future development of each tradition. For the religions are not rock-like entities, 'the same yesterday, today and for ever', but are on the contrary historical movements undergoing continuous change and growth. As living organisms they interact with their environment; and in the unified world of modern communications the other religions form part of the environment with which each is in interaction. It does not follow that the religions will eventually flow together into a single world faith – indeed that seems highly improbable. But it does mean that further thinking within each tradition is likely to be done, to an increasing extent, in the light of the variant options opened up by awareness of the other traditions.

In many respects Christianity and Buddhism stand at opposite ends of the religious spectrum, and any kind of fruitful interaction between them might at first glance seem to be unlikely. However, Dr de Silva challenges that assumption. He is concerned with one of the most conspicuous Christian–Buddhist contrasts: that whereas Christianity has traditionally taught the existence and the immortal life of the individual soul, Buddhism has traditionally taught that there is no permanent soul and that salvation consists in transcending individual selfhood. Starting here, Dr de Silva proceeds to look beneath the surface, and finds hidden depths of analogous insight. He draws out what might daringly be called the Christian-Buddhist concept of *anatta-pneuma*, or non-egocentric mutuality. In the light of this idea human selves are not seen as atomic entities, permanently excluding one another, but as parts of a living system of inter-personal relationships, within which their separating walls of egoity may ultimately be transcended. Dr de Silva develops the idea on several levels, social as well as theological; but I must leave the reader to pursue this intriguing conception for himself in the following chapters. I would only add that, in my view, this is the kind of exploration in which the next main phase of religious thinking will almost certainly consist. The period of the separate elaboration of the particular traditions, each without regard to the others, is now probably substantially over, and is already giving place to a rethinking of religious issues within each tradition in the context of dialogue with other traditions.

The author of this book is Director of the Study Centre for Religion and Society at Colombo, and is one of the foremost contemporary Christian practitioners of dialogue with Buddhists in Sri Lanka (Ceylon). His journal *Dialogue* has become an important forum of inter-religious discussion. Dr de Silva is also the author of several studies of the Theravāda Buddhism of Sri Lanka and of particular aspects of Buddhist and Christian belief. His present book now speaks to a wider circle, making available some very significant insights gained in dialogue with Buddhists, so that these can now begin to fertilise Christian thinking in the west as well as in Sri Lanka.

JOHN HICK

Department of Theology
The University of Birmingham

Preface to the First Edition

The self has been a perennial problem in religious, sociological and philosophical thought, and there has been a search for authentic selfhood, in which theologians as well as Marxists, philosophers as well as hippies, have been involved. In this book I have made an attempt, firstly, to define, making use of Buddhist and Christian insights, a form of 'selfhood' in terms of the mutuality of personal relations, so that the unit of personal life is not the egocentric 'I' but the mutuality of 'I' and 'Thou', and secondly, I have indicated the social relevance of this view. Against the view that the self is an isolated individual having an immortal soul, a notion which Buddhism emphatically rejects, I have set the view that authentic 'selfhood' is what is constituted in inter-personal relationships apart from which no person exists. The person as subject is only a derivative aspect of the person-in-relation.

The Buddhist doctrine of *anattā*, with its rejection of the notion of the immortal soul within man, serves to dispel the illusion of the egocentric 'I', which is, as the Buddha taught, the root cause of all evil. I have argued in this book that this insight which comes from Buddhism is in harmony with the biblical understanding of man. While Buddhism is emphatic on the *anattā* aspect, Christianity is emphatic on the relational aspect which can be best signified by the biblical term *pneuma*, or spirit. By bringing these two emphases together, I have attempted to define authentic selfhood as *anattā-pneuma* – egoless mutuality or non-egocentric relationality. For the Christian *anattā* has meaning only in the context of mutuality.

On the basis of this anthropology, I have sought to offer a solution to the theological problem which is posed by Buddhism but which Christianity too has to face: the problem of denying the self or soul without falling into the error of nihilism (*ucchedadiṭṭhi*) and of affirming self-identity without falling into the opposite error of eternalism (*sassatadiṭṭhi*). This is however not a matter of merely theological interest; it has its implications for a sociological understanding of man's search for community and the common human aspirations and responsibilities in the quest for a peaceful and hopeful future for mankind, so powerfully reflected in Marxist-Maoist ideologies. This study therefore has a practical end in view.

Thus, this is not a book on the comparative study of religion as the reader might expect it to be. I have not attempted to compare the Buddhist and Christian teachings about man and to show how one is superior or inferior to the other. My interest is not in comparing one religion with another, however useful this may be academically, but to see how they can be related to one another; how the insights of one religion can fertilise another religion and how the spiritual resources of religions and ideologies can be harnessed for the common good of man. This I believe is very important in a world where there is a growing appreciation of religious truths wherever they are found – in religions or ideologies – and an increasing degree of practical co-operation between people of different persuasions.

I do not share the fear of many people, particularly Christians, that the acknowledgement of spiritual truths in other religions will weaken one's commitment to one's own faith; rather I am convinced that one's own faith can be deepened and broadened by a sympathetic and intelligent understanding of the faith of others. This has been my experience in my study of Buddhism. There are truths in Buddhism that can be absorbed or adapted into Christianity and which can fertilise and enrich a Christian's own faith. Some of these can be a corrective to certain deviations from biblical truths. An integration of Buddhist terms and thought-forms into Christianity can also help Christianity to be more indigenous and also more deeply rooted in the soil of this land. Furthermore it can facilitate Buddhist-Christian dialogue and help people of these two faiths to overcome prejudices and misunderstandings of the past and understand each other better.

A number of Buddhist terms and concepts have come to have a real meaning for me in the context of my own faith, and as I looked at Christian teaching through Buddhist eyes, as it were, I have been able to see dimensions of truth which I had hitherto not seen. This is particularly true with regard to the doctrine of *anattā*. It is a doctrine which dispels the egoistic view of selfhood centred on the concept of an immortal soul, which, as I hope to show, is not a biblical idea at all. Hence the Buddhist doctrine of *anattā* serves to remind Christians of a truly biblical insight which they have lost track of under the influence of Greek philosophy. When this *anattā* notion is brought into relation with the concept of *pneuma* we are able to define a form of selfhood as stated above, and work out its implications for an understanding of the new man, his religious and social responsibilities.

The question may be asked: what right have I to use terms and ideas that belong to Buddhism to express Christian truths? The answer is simple: I am doing what is inevitable in a multi-religious context and what most religious teachers have done. For instance, the Buddha took over terms, concepts, beliefs and practices from Hinduism and other sources and grafted them on to his own system of thought. Numerous examples could be given: the most obvious is the term *Karma* and its corollary rebirth. The *pañcasīla* has roots in Jainism, and the four *Brahma Vihāras*, according to the *Jātaka* commentary, were practised long before the rise of Buddhism. In the *Brahma Vagga* of the *Dhammapada* the term Brahmin is used to describe the holy life instead of the word Arahant, and in the *Tevijja Sutta* the Buddha speaks of Union with Brahmā in theistic terms. As C. A. F. Rhys Davids says, 'There was not much in the metaphysics and principles of Gautama which cannot be found in one or other of the orthodox systems, and a great deal of his morality could be matched from earlier or later Hindu books.' These were taken over by the Buddha and *'adopted'*, *'enlarged'*, *'ennobled'* and *'systematised.'* (*Buddhism* (London: Lutterworth Press, 1922), pp. 83 and 84).

When we turn to the New Testament we see how its writers pressed into the service of the gospel words, concepts, and symbols taken from Greek philosophy, Mystery Religions and Gnosticism, in order to make sense of the Christian message in the context in which it was proclaimed. This kind of thing is bound to happen in the multi-religious context in which we live today, and I believe it will contribute towards the emerging world community.

There is a growing body of opinion within Christianity that its theology is shop-soiled and needs drastic revision in order, firstly, to re-root it in basic biblical teaching, secondly, to bring it into harmony with new insights and modes of thought coming from other faiths, ideologies and modern science and, thirdly, to relate it to social realities. Such a transformation is, I believe, taking place not only in Christianity, but also in other religions. What I have attempted is to help this process of transformation of Christian thinking. However, theological thinking in order to be meaningful and relevant must be contextual. The context of this book is Buddhism. I have therefore identified the problem and examined the traditional solutions offered by both religions and attempted to suggest a more satisfactory solution from the *anattā-pneuma* point of view. I have also indicated in the last chapter how the anthropology that emerges from this study can have a sociological relevance also, in relation to Marxist-Maoist ideologies.

I am deeply grateful to the Rev. Cyril Premawardhana, M.A., B.D., S.T.M., Director of the Department of Buddhist studies, Theological College of Lanka, for reading the manuscript and giving valuable suggestions; to Mr Shelton Wirasinha, B.A., and Miss J. F. Newsham B.SC., for reading the proofs and to many friends, Buddhist and Christian, with whom I had the privilege of discussing various points in this book.

LYNN A. DE SILVA

The Study Centre for Religion and Society
Colombo, Sri Lanka

Preface to the Library of Philosophy and Religion Edition

Arnold Toynbee once said that future historians will consider the meeting between Buddhism and Christianity at their deepest levels as the most important single event of this century. This meeting, or what we prefer to call dialogue, has already begun and the results have been amazing and illuminating. This book is the outcome of such dialogue between Buddhists and Christians in Sri Lanka. Out of a population of a little over twelve and a half million people Buddhists of the Theravāda tradition count 67.3%, Hindus 17.6%, Christians 7.9% (including R.C. 7.1%) and Muslims 7.1%. This book indicates new directions in Asian theological thinking that are emerging as a result of dialogue at depth between Buddhists and Christians.

I am very grateful to Professor John Hick for selecting this book for the Library of Philosophy and Religion, of which he is the General Editor. On reading his book *Death and Eternal Life*, which was published after my book, I discovered that our minds have been running along somewhat parallel lines and what he says in his book agrees very much with what I say in my book. This is particularly with regard to the *anattā-pneuma* theory. I think that his own position about the self as ego and the self as personal is essentially similar to mine and that our discussions mutually support each other. His book has helped me very much in preparing this new edition. Among the new material added to this new edition is a section on the 'Replica' theory which I owe to Professor Hick.

I am very grateful to the publishers for their encouragement and to Rev. John H. Grice M.A., for preparing the manuscript for resetting and for reading the final proofs.

LYNN A. DE SILVA

1 Introduction

Modern studies in biology, psychology and physiology are all agreed in rendering incredible the doctrine of the immortality of the soul. Of all the great religions, it is Buddhism that has come out most strongly against this false notion. The doctrine of *anattā*, which teaches that there is no immortal soul in man, is the bedrock of Buddhist teaching. Modern biblical scholarship also has now come round to the view that in the Bible there is no notion of an immortal soul inhabiting the body. At the same time the popular Christian belief of the resurrection of the flesh into a heavenly world, conceived more or less in physical terms, has been discredited. Any eternalistic notions about man therefore are ruled out.

Does the eclipse of the idea of the soul then lead to a nihilistic view? Neither Buddhism nor Christianity succumbs to such a view. Both religions teach that there is a future life, a hereafter beyond the grave. This raises some vital questions: What is it that survives death? What is its nature? What is its relation to the physical body? If there is no soul how can we speak of survival after death?

Both Buddhism and Christianity have their own answers to these questions. While Buddhism throughout the ages has been true to its scriptural teaching of the doctrine of *anattā*, traditional Christianity has moved away from the biblical teaching about man, into acceptance of the doctrine of the immortal soul. Thus, Theravāda Buddhism and Christianity are considered to be two religions that stand in direct opposition to each other. Buddhism is considered to be an atheistic or rather a non-theistic religion, denying both the idea of God and the soul, while Christianity, in contrast, affirms both these. Polemical and apologetic writings have emphasised this polarity and widened the gap between these two faiths. While it is granted that there is some common ground between the two religions on the ethical plane, it is asserted that on the level of fundamental doctrines it is hard to find anything in common.

This mutual exclusiveness on the doctrinal level is particularly marked, it is held, in the teachings of the two religions about man.

In this regard, Buddhism is supposed to deny precisely what Christianity affirms; one teaches the doctrine of no-soul (*anattā*) while the other teaches, it is assumed, just the opposite – the doctrine of the immortal soul. In this book I have called in question this assumption and have taken pains to show that there is no notion of an immortal soul in the Bible; rather there is much in the biblical view of man that is in accord with the Buddhist doctrine of *anattā*.

In Chapters 2 to 7 I have explained and examined the doctrine of *anattā*, focusing attention on the question of self-identity in relation to the theory of *karma* and rebirth and the attainment of *Nirvāna*, the ultimate goal. It is here that we are faced with crucial problems.

On the one hand the negation of the self according to the theory of *anattā* seems to amount to a doctrine of nihilism; on the other hand the belief in *karma* and rebirth, which in a sense affirms the identity and continuity of the self, seems to amount to a doctrine of eternalism. But Buddhism emphasises that it does not fall into the errors of either nihilism (*ucchedavāda*), or eternalism (*sassatavāda*). This assertion constitutes a major problem. How can you reconcile the doctrine of *anattā*, which denies the self, with the doctrine of *karma* and rebirth, which affirms the identity and continuity of the self? To save what it holds as an empirical and psychological truth which has a moral significance, Buddhism rightly rejects the notion of an immortal soul; to save what it holds to be a necessity of justice it retains the belief in *karma* and rebirth. How can these two conflicting views be maintained without falling into the errors of nihilism and eternalism?

This question comes up most acutely in relation to the concept of *Nirvāna*, which is described as a state of supreme bliss. If in reality there is no self, who is it who attains *Nirvāna* and experiences happiness? Is *Nirvāna* total annihilation or eternal bliss? This problem has vexed the minds of Buddhist thinkers from very early times. Theravāda Buddhism has claimed that the doctrine of *anattā* is consistent with the belief in rebirth and has sought to explain this paradox in terms of the classic formula, *na ca so, na ca añño* – 'the person who is born is neither the same nor is he another.' Some scholars have argued that *anattā* and rebirth are inconsistent and have rejected the latter as not belonging to the true teaching of the Buddha. According to them, *anattā* is literally a total denial of the self; death is the final stroke of extinction and there is nothing that survives death. Others have argued that the Buddha never categorically denied the self; what he denied was the false or unauthentic (*olārika*) self and not the authentic self. In between these extremes one finds sophisticated explanations of the term *anattā* and efforts to smuggle in the idea of the soul in disguise.

Although there are difficulties in the Buddhist doctrine of *anattā*, it enshrines a truth about the nature of man, which is in accord with modern physical sciences and which is a corrective to the deviation in Christian thinking we have noted. This truth I believe, helps us to understand, more deeply and contextually, the biblical teaching about man.

In Chapter 8 I have set out in a summary form the biblical teaching about man and shown that there is no support for the idea of an immortal soul in the Bible. I have also attempted to express the biblical teaching about man in a Buddhist framework of thought. Since this is a crucial chapter, a summary of it would be helpful to the reader.

The idea of an immortal soul is certainly a firmly established traditional belief of Christians, but it is a belief that has entered Christian thinking through the influence of Greek philosophy and is altogether alien to what the Bible teaches about the nature and destiny of man. The chief emphasis in Greek thought as it is found in Orphism and developed by Plato, particularly in the Socratic dialogue on death and immortality of the soul, is upon a dualism of body and soul in the human person. The body is mortal and is subject to corruption, decay and final extinction at death. The soul on the contrary is immortal, not subject to decay and death and will continue in unending and eternal existence independent of the body. It is this strain of thought that influenced Christian thinking in later days. But this is quite contrary to the distinctive Hebraic-Christian strain of thought that runs through the Bible, which stresses resurrection as opposed to immortality. However, the recent recovery of 'biblical theology' in Protestant thought – a major trend in the twentieth century which reaffirms biblical faith in the context of historical criticism of the scriptures – has shown quite convincingly that there is no dualistic notion of the self as composed of a body and an immortal soul in the Bible as is found in Greek philosophy. There is hardly anything in the Bible to support a doctrine of the immortality of the soul. On the contrary, one finds in the Bible much that is in accord with the Buddhist doctrine of *anattā*. It can be confidently said that in the Bible there is no notion of an immortal soul existing independently as an eternal immutable and perdurable entity, which inhabits the body and escapes it at death. It is this notion that Buddhism rejects in no uncertain terms, and on this point there is a fundamental agreement between Buddhism and biblical theology, so much so that it is possible to state a biblical view of man employing Buddhist categories of thought.

According to the biblical view, man is a psycho-physical unity, of 'soul' (*psyche*) and 'flesh' (*sarx*). This bears a close resemblance to the Buddhist analysis of man in terms of *nāma* (name) and *rūpa* (form). *Psyche*, like *nāma*, corresponds to the psychical aspect of man, which represents more or less those processes that come within the field of psychology, and *sarx*, like *rūpa*, corresponds to the physical processes with which the biologist is concerned. Both the Buddhist and the biblical views of man agree that there is no distinguishable, immortal soul within this psycho-physical (*nāma-rūpa*) aggregation which constitutes a person.

Alternately, taking the five-fold analysis of personality (the *Pañcakkhanda* theory) into *rūpa* (matter), *vedanā* (sensation or feeling), *saññā* (perceptions), *saṃkhārā* (mental formations) and *viññaṇā* (consciousness), we could say from the biblical point of view in respect of each of these, as the Buddha does in his second sermon (the *anattā-lakkhaṇa sutta*), 'that is *an-attā*' – not-self, or not-the-self. That is to say that none of the aggregates can be identified with the self or soul, nor do they together constitute the self. According to the biblical teaching, in whatever way you may analyse man – either according to Buddhist psychology or modern psychology – there is nothing in man that can be identified as a soul-entity, nor do all the component parts put together constitute a person as an independent self-existent being.

If, as has been argued in this book, the concept of an immortal soul is foreign to the biblical understanding of man, then biblical theology will be faced with the same problem as Buddhism. The question is: Can we find a satisfactory explanation of the meaning of selfhood or personality which provides for the negation of the self that does not amount to nihilism (*ucchedadiṭṭhi*) and for the affirmation of the self that does not amount to eternalism (*sassatadiṭṭhi*)? My contention is that from the Christian point of view the answer to this question is to be found in the understanding of selfhood as consisting in the mutuality of personal relationships; in the mutually interacting 'I – Thou' and not in the exclusive 'I'. This is an insight that has come to the fore in recent biblical theology and is affirmed even by thinkers who are not biblical scholars or Christians. Karl Marx, for instance, who was a Jew, gave expression to this biblical insight when he said, 'Man is an ensemble of social relations'.

The most important word that describes this relationship is 'spirit' (*pneuma* in the N.T., *ruach* in the O.T.), which I have discussed in Chapter 9. This word has almost exclusively been treated integrally with the Divine Spirit or Holy Spirit. But 'spirit' has to do with the human spirit as well as the Divine Spirit, the two being implicates of each other. The New Testament writers make a distinction by using this term with or without the definite article. In the former case, it denotes the Divine Person and, in the latter case, a human experience. Man is 'spirit' only in relation to God who is Spirit. God is eternal (*Amata*) and man shares this deathless quality with the Eternal in relationship with Him. In the Bible, the term 'spirit' functions descriptively as the central core concept of the authentic 'self', which exists only in a relationship. It is at this point that we find a fundamental difference between the Buddhist and Christian views of the self and it is therefore essential that this term 'spirit' be rightly understood.

A biblically-based new assessment of the meaning of 'spirit', as the personal-communal dimension of man, is a theological necessity in our search for a solution for the problem with which we are concerned. Primarily, 'spirit' stands for the multi-dimensional unity of life; the all-inclusive totality in which the whole contains the parts in distinction and unity. It is the co-humanity in which the 'I' and the 'Thou' meet inherently, making for genuine self-identity without the implications of a discrete soul-entity; it signifies the personal-communal relationship in which alone a person exists. No individual exists without participation and no personal being exists without 'communal being'. To be is to be related. The individual is a fact of existence in so far as he steps into a living relationship with other individuals. In thus stepping into a relationship with others, an individual can reach beyond himself. 'Spirit' is thus the category of self-transcendence. In transcending one's self one can cease to be a self, i.e. realise that one is *anattā*. But selfhood is always being fulfilled by being transcended. It is by transcending the self that self can be negated and affirmed. This is possible only in an 'I – Thou' relationship. In this 'I – Thou' relationship is to be found the true meaning of *anattā*, which denies the 'soul' without yielding to a nihilistic view, and which affirms authentic selfhood without yielding to an eternalistic view. In such a view the doctrine of *anattā* is not rejected; rather the spiritual meaning implied in it is preserved. The spiritual meaning of *anattā* is the realisation that by oneself one is nothing and that it is by self-negation or denying oneself that one's true self can be discovered in a relationship.

This understanding of *anattā* and *pneuma* enables us to see these two concepts not in contrast but in combination – *anattā-pneuma*. Each is enriched and deepened by the other. From the psychophysical point of view *anattā* means the rejection of an immortal soul within man. This is a corrective to the wrong notion that has invaded popular Christian thinking. However, the five-fold (*pañcakkhandha*) analysis seems to reduce man to a psychosomatic organism. But *pneuma* points to a dimension that cannot be exhausted by such an analysis; it signifies that extra dimension of finite life which is constitutive of authentic being that makes a man more than a bundle of aggregates or an unusually complex animal.

From the ethico-religious point of view *anattā* means non-attachment, particularly to the notion of a soul. Relinquishing of self is therefore a primary religious concern for the attainment of which Buddhism has developed an ethical discipline, unparalleled in any other religion. But, over-stressing this aspect can make man's religious quest highly individualistic, leading to isolation and a socially irrelevant way of life. *Pneuma* affirms the social dimension. It signifies the fact that man is by nature a 'communal' being. Authentic being is not what one attains for oneself but something that is shared and found in relationships.

From the experiential point of view *anattā* implies a realisation of absolute self-emptying. That realisation is *Nirvāna*. The Christian view is that this goal is achieved in communion. *Pneuma* signifies that capacity for transcending oneself and losing oneself in communion with Reality. In communion exclusive self-contained individuality disappears, but selfhood is being fulfilled by being transcended. It is by the realisation that one is *anattā*, that realisation of perfect communion is possible. It is a state in which the ego, the separate 'I' is negated without personality being obliterated. (It is important that the reader bears in mind the three senses in which I have used the word *anattā*.)

The question still remains: What is it that continues after death? The Christian answer, in contrast to reincarnation or rebirth, is in terms of resurrection. This question is discussed in Chapter 10. Christianity speaks of the 'Resurrection of the Body'. This does not mean a fleshy resurrection, or reconstituted corpses. If we accept the fact of *anattā*, the finitude, transience and mortality of man – then we have to accept the fact that death is the end of existence, the horizon that shuts off the future. We cannot think of man having a self-generative power as the doctrine of *karma* implies. If *anattā* is real there cannot be natural survival after death. Survival is possible only if God re-creates a new being. This is the truth of resurrection. It is an act of God by which He creates 'a spiritual body'. To explain what this means I have employed the 'replica' theory, according to which at the moment of death God creates 'an exact psycho-physical "replica" of the deceased person'. It is a new creation. Because this is a re-creation, the spiritual body is not the same as the self that existed in the earthly body (*na ca so*). But because the recreated spiritual body is an 'exact psycho-physical "replica" of the deceased person' the re-created body is not a different one (*na ca añño*). The doctrine of Resurrection or the theory of 'replication' offers, I believe, a way out of the difficulty of believing in the hereafter while accepting the fact of *anattā*.

Thus we can speak of the identity and continuity of the self here and hereafter, through progressive sanctification, without falling into the errors of either nihilism or eternalism. This is an important idea, which I have set out in Chapter 11. I believe it provides a satisfactory alternative to the doctrine of reincarnation. The identity and continuity of the self is an identity and continuity in relationships, which death does not sever. 'We pass from death into life', says St John, 'because we love the brethren' (1 John 3:14). Love is eternal, because God is Love and he who abides in Love has entered the sphere of the Eternal. This sphere of life begins here and now and continues in the hereafter. And it is in this sphere that a person is progressively sanctified until he reaches perfection.

The idea of progressive sanctification after death contradicts the double predestination theory, according to which the moment of death is decisive and irrevocably determines one's fate, and thereafter one is predestined to go either to hell or to heaven. Elsewhere I have argued that this is a mistaken notion which must be discarded as not in keeping with biblical teaching.

There is convincing evidence in the New Testament to support the notion of progressive sanctification after death rather than the belief that at the moment of death one is transmuted immediately into a perfect state or condemned to eternal damnation.

How does progressive sanctification take place? It is, as has been suggested, through individualisation and participation. This is a principle of great significance. According to this principle, no individual exists without participation or communion. Persons grow only in the communion of personal encounter. The more a person enters into communion, the more he individualises himself and becomes a person. Individualisation in the true sense of the word is not through separation but through participation. Separation leads to extinction and loss of self; participation leads to fulness of being. It is when participation reaches the perfect form which we call 'communion' that individualisation reaches its perfect form which we call 'person'. But this perfection is never reached in this life. It is possible only in the consummation, in the Kingdom of God.

This brings us to Chapter 12. We might describe the Kingdom of God as the Divine Commonwealth or simply the Community of Love. The word 'Kingdom' implies community, and God is love. It embraces all dimensions of being – the individual and social, the historical and the trans-historical. This is in agreement with the multi-dimensional unity of life and the personal communal nature of being. Thus the Community of Love has a double quality embracing the particular and the universal in such a way that the individual is transcended in a social reality and the historical in a trans-historical reality. Thus all aspects of being find fulfilment in the Kingdom. That which upholds and maintains the double quality is love, which is the highest manifestation of Spirit.

In the Kingdom of God individualisation reaches its perfect form, which we call 'person', and participation reaches its perfect form, which we call 'communion'. Herein we have the answer to the quest for self-negation without the implication of nihilism, as well as for self-realisation without the implication of eternalism. There can be no communion without participation, and this means that perfect communion implies a differentiation of individual centres of participation. The underlying principle is that union or communion differentiates by negating exclusive individuality and perfecting personality. Perfect communion implies the 'extinction' of the self, i.e. the dying-out of separate individuality, by one wholly participating in the other. In this the principle of self-negation underlying the concepts of *anattā* and *Nirvāna* is fulfilled. In communion, self-contained, self-conscious individuality disappears. On the other hand, communion implies a differentiation and, as such, genuine self-identity is preserved. Eternal life in the Kingdom is participation in the individuality-negating, but personality-fulfilling, love.

It is love alone that is capable of uniting in such a way as to negate exclusive individuality and complete and fulfil personality. The loss of self-contained individuality in participation, which constitutes the fulfilment of personality in communion, is the essence of the experience of love, which is the highest manifestation of *pneuma* and which constitutes the basis for the mutuality of the 'I' and the 'Thou'. The life of love is a life of mutual giving and receiving, of the individualisation and participation, of self-loss and self-gain. And this is an experience we have all around us in marriage, friendship and service.

Thus the destiny of man is intimately related to the nature of man. What we are essentially, we become finally. Through progressive sanctification man grows towards the End.

In the End we shall be fully persons and cease completely to be individuals. We shall retain our differentiation as persons, without that differentiation being expressed in the exclusiveness of individuality. We shall retain identity within a complete harmony. The relationship in which we live on earth will be fulfilled in the Kingdom of God, except that the implications of exclusiveness in the relationship will have ceased to have meaning.

Such a state is possible because man is related to a power or reality 'above' or 'beyond' himself, i.e. beyond his material life. This reality is referred to in different religions as Brahma, Allah, 'Buddha' – life, or even *Nirvāna*. Religion is therefore an expression of man's relation to the limits of his own existence. That ultimate frontier of human existence, in whichever way religions may conceive it, is what the word 'God' signifies. In Chapter 13 I have argued that without a Reality above, behind and within the passing flux of conditioned things, in which man can go beyond himself and lose himself, the concept of *anattā* ends in a nihilism.

It is my contention that if *anattā* is real, God is necessary; it is in relation to the reality of God that the reality of *anattā* can be meaningful. Because man is *anattā*, God is indispensable; because man is absolutely *anattā*, God is absolutely necessary. The conditioned (*saṃkhata*) man has nothing to hope for unless there is an Unconditioned Reality (*asaṃkhata*) and it is in relation to the Unconditioned (God) that the full depth and significance of *anattā* can be understood.

To put it in another way: if man is absolutely *anattā* the hypothesis of the unconditioned or some such other hypothesis becomes absolutely necessary if the error of nihilism (*ucchedadiṭṭhi*) is to be avoided. Apart from the unconditioned reality there can be no emancipation for that which is conditioned; all that can be expected is total annihilation. On the other hand if extinction is not the final end, the ultimate reality becomes necessary. This is because finitude – the realm of the born, the become, the made, the compounded – cannot contain by its own intrinsic power the reality that negates and transcends finitude.

The study of man is not just an academic subject nor one of mere religious or philosophical interest. Marxists as well as followers of other secular ideologies are as much involved in the search for authentic selfhood – for the 'new man' – as theologians and philosophers. What is involved in the study is the discovery of man's essential or authentic being and its implications for his total life, religious and social. In this context the discovery of the *anattā* dimension of man, supplemented by the *pneuma* dimension, is very significant.

The true person is the selfless person, one who realises that he is by himself a nobody, that he is *na-attā*, and that his real worth is to be found in his relationships. This implies a selfless commitment to the service of man, a collective life and a socially-orientated work-style. This discovery of the 'new man', I believe, will go a long way to promote better undertanding between religions and the so-called secular ideologies, which are unfortunately considered to be in opposition to one another. It will also promote better understanding between people of different faiths. In the last chapter I have indicated some ways in which we can pursue this line of thought further.

2 Soul Theories

The doctrine of *anattā* forms the subject of the Buddha's second sermon – the so-called *anattalakkhaṇa sutta* – after hearing which it is said that his first five disciples attained to the state of perfection (*arahathood*). It is considered to be one of the main corner-stones, if not the main one, upon which the edifice of the Buddha's teaching is built.

Etymologically the word *anattā* consists of the negative prefix *an* and *atta* (Sanskrit *ātman*), meaning no-self, no-soul or non-substantiality. The term *an-atta* therefore implies a non-atta or non-self theory which negates other *attā* or *ātman* theories. There were prior to and during the time of the Buddha many *ātman* or soul theories. It is in contrast to them that the Buddha preached his new doctrine of no-self. Therefore a brief consideration of these theories will help our investigation considerably, and provide a background to understanding the doctrine of *anattā*.

I. VEDĀNTIC BACKGROUND

The Sanskrit word *ātman* is found in the earliest Vedic hymns, though one cannot be certain of its derivation and meaning. It is sometimes said to have meant 'breath' in the sense of 'life' and could be compared to the Greek *psychē*[1]. In this sense the sun is called the *ātman* of all that moves or stands still, and the *soma* drink is called the *ātman* of the Vedic sacrifices. This *ātman* or breath-life was thought of as some vitality that could leave the body and return to it again. In this connection, *manas* (mind), was used as a synonym[2] and this association gradually developed, giving rise to more well-marked conceptions as we find in the Upanishads.

The central concept of Vedāntic thought can be briefly stated as follows. The fundamental character of Reality, the Eternal, the Absolute, is expressed in the word *Brahman*. The manifestation of *Brahman* was sometimes personified and called *Brahmā*, meaning

God or the Great Self. *Brahman* is *Sat, Cit, Ānanda* (Absolute Being, Absolute Consciousness, Absolute Bliss). Every human being had in him a part of *Brahman*, which was called *ātman* or the little self. *Brahman* and *ātman* are one, and it is only ignorance (*avidyā*) that prevents one from realising this truth. Salvation (*moksha*) consists in removing the veil of ignorance and realising this oneness of the *ātman* with the *Brahman*. This idea is expressed in the famous words '*tat tvam asi*' ('that thou art'). Thus the *ātman* came to be thought of as an eternal immutable substance, free from the vicissitudes of change and decay.

In the course of time, however, various theories grew round this notion of the *ātman*. Many of these theories are mentioned and refuted in the *Brahmajāla Sutta*, which is supposed to deal with every possible theory concerning the *atta* and the universe treated from every point of view, positive, negative and both.[3] From a statement made in this Sutta, to the effect that some teachers, who held soul theories, wriggled like eels and refused to give a clear answer, it can be inferred that there was a considerable amount of controversy about the self or soul centring round such questions as: What is the origin of the *attā*? What is its nature? What is its location? How can it be known? What is its destiny?

2.   ORIGIN OF THE ATTA

Regarding the origin of the *attā*, some held that it was eternal and had arisen without a cause (*ādhicca-samuppanna*). Pakudha Kaccāyana, a contemporary of the Buddha, for instance, held that there were seven eternal elements, namely, *āpo* (fluidity), *tējo* (fire), *vāyo* (wind), *paṭhavī* (earth), *sukha* (pleasures), *dukkha* (pain) and *jīva* (soul). These elements are neither created nor moulded. They are immutable. Hence a person cannot be killed. If a person is pierced with a sword it only passes through the interspace of the elements forming the body. At death the body is dissolved into seven eternal elements.

Another contemporary of the Buddha, Makkhali Gosala, the founder of the Ājivaka sect, held the theory called *samsāra visuddhi*, according to which all beings were subject to a fixed series of existences (*samsāra*) from the lowliest to the highest. *Samsāra* was to him a cycle of reanimation, a process through which everyone had to pass until he was completely purified and freed from misery, when the cycle came to an end. Like a ball of thread it had a fixed term. Nothing could be done to change this course of natural purification. Good or bad deeds have no effect on one's destiny. The Sāṃkhyas also taught the doctrine of the eternal existence of a plurality of souls on the one hand, and also of a unique pervasive substantial matter on the other. These were all classed as eternalistic views (*sassata vāda*), according to which the soul had no beginning in time and hence no end.

3. NATURE OF THE ATTA

There is evidence of much speculation about the nature of the *ātman*. Some described it in spacial terms. For instance the Ājīvakas seem to have held the view that the *ātman* was octagonal or globular is shape, five hundred yojanas (about 3500 miles) in extent and blue in colour.[4] Sometimes these spatial terms have been used metaphorically. The soul is referred to as 'more minute than the minute, greater than the great.'[5] The Jainas held that the soul (*jīva*), which is identifiable with life, is finite and has a definite size and weight, though variable according to circumstances, and that this *jīva* is not only in human beings but in everything else in the world – in animals, insects and plants. When Mahāvīra, the founder of Jainism, was asked whether the *jīva* was identical with the body or different from it, he is said to have given the paradoxical answer that it is both identical and different, probably meaning that the soul was identical with the body from one point of view and different from another point of view.[6] The Jainas held that the soul was intrinsically omniscient, though cluttered up by the material particles of karma. When these karmic particles cease to be, by the complete extinction of *karma*, then the soul shines in its natural and intrinsic lustre. The Upanishads speak of the *ātman* as being conscious, and as such, if it so desires, it can be conscious of enjoyment with women, chariots and relations.[7] The *ātman* is identified with the body and also with the self in a dream-state.[8] This *ātman* is free from death (*vimrāyuh*), free from sorrow (*visokhah*) and has real thoughts (*satyasamkalpah*).[9]

If one could know the size of the soul, then one could also locate it. Thus there is the notion that the self, as something physical, is of the size of a thumb and is located in the cavity of the heart. There are numerous channels radiating from the heart, through any of which the soul may leave during deep sleep. It may also pass on to immortality from one aperture at the top of the head.[10]

About how the soul can be known different views have been expressed. There were some thinkers who held that the *ātman* could be known in the usual ways of knowing by the senses, that it could be empirically perceived and conceived by the rational processes of thinking.[11] The middle and late Upanishads, however, seem to agree with Yājnavalkya, that the soul is unknowable by any process of reasoning. Because the *ātman* is subtler than the subtle, it is inconceivable and cannot be known by the intellect;[12] because it is hidden within all things and does not shine forth it cannot be seen by the sense organs; but it can be perceived by awakened intuition achieved through the purification of knowledge.[13]

4. DESTINY OF THE ATTA

As regards the destiny of the soul, the general idea was that it could be separated from the body like the sword from the scabbard, or the fibre from the stalk of grass, and exist after death in a conscious or unconscious state, the final destiny being union with Brahman.

All these views of the *ātman* can be classed as eternalist views (*sassata vāda*). One of the Upanishadic passages describes the eternal indestructible soul as follows:

> The wise one (i.e. the soul, the *ātman*, the self) is not born, nor dies.
> This one has not come from anywhere, has not become anyone.
> Unborn, constant, eternal, primeval, this one
> is not slain when the body is slain.
>   If the slayer think to slay,
>   If the slain think himself slain,
>   Both these understand not.
>   This one slays not, nor is slain.[14]

Summing up the Hindu thought about the soul S. Rādha-krishnan says:

> If there is one doctrine more than another which is characteristic of Hindu thought, it is the belief that there is an interior depth to the human soul which, in its essence, is uncreated and deathless, and absolutely real.[15]

5. ANNIHILATIONIST VIEWS

In opposition to the eternalist views there were also annihilationist views (*uccheda vāda*). Ajita Kesakambali, another contemporary of the Buddha, was one of the outstanding nihilists. He held that there is no life after death; a man consists of four elements and when he dies and is cremated, the elements return to their corresponding mass of great elements and he is completely annihilated. Nothing survives death. So there is no purpose in trying to earn merit by doing good deeds, performing sacrifices or rendering service to one's parents or others.

Some annihilationists denied the existence of an *ātman*, while others said that even if there was an *ātman*, it ceased to exist, if not at death in this world, either in the world of sense (*kāma loka*), or in the world of form (*rūpa loka*), or in one of the stages of the formless world (*arūpa loka*). They seem to have admitted a dualism of body and soul, more or less as a concession to the eternalists, but they said that, although the soul may continue to live for some time after the death of the body, sooner or later it is completely annihilated.

These views had a practical bearing on morality. Some said that since the *ātman* was eternal, nothing could be done to improve or degrade its condition, and therefore, good or bad deeds were of no significance. Some like Purana Kassapa were amoralists and advocated inaction. They held that if there was no life after death merit and demerit could do no good or harm. They were known as *Akiriyavādins* and were indifferent to morals. Such theories as these led to lax living (*kāmasukhallikānuyoga*). On the other hand, some who believed that there is an *ātman* in everyone said that it was affected by what one does and prescribed ethical means to achieve purity of the soul by which one could attain liberation. The stress on ethical discipline led some, like the *Ājīvakas*, to advocate extreme forms of self-mortification (*attakilamathānuyoga*) as an essential means of gaining salvation. Thus, bound up with the conflicting views of the soul, tending towards either eternalistic or nihilistic extremes, there were conflicting views about morality, tending towards either moralistic or amoralistic extremes.

Whether all these views were in actual existence, or whether some of them were later inventions added to make the picture of the 'net' (*jālā*)[16] complete, is not certain. Some of them however, can be identified with the actual teachings of some schools of thought about which we have some evidence. Whatever it be, it is against the background of such theories, existent or invented, that the Theravādins developed their doctrine of *anattā*, as found in the Pali scriptures.

3 The No-Soul Theory

Whatever be the theories about the *ātman* held by the various thinkers during the time of the Buddha and thereafter, the Buddhist doctrine of *anattā*, as preserved in the Theravāda tradition, contradicts them all in an all-embracing sweep. Nyānaponika Thera, a German monk who lived in Sri Lanka for many years, gives expression to the Theravāda view when he describes 'belief in a self, a soul, or an eternal substance of any description' as 'the deepest and most obstinate delusion in man.'[1] The argument against the *ātman* theories is two-fold – analytical and ethical.

I. THE ANALYTICAL ARGUMENT

(a) *Nāma-rūpa analysis*
In the first place Buddhism examines the various aspects of the so-called person (*puggala*) and contends, by minutely analysing them, that none of them can be identified with the *ātman*, and that no *ātman* can be found when the person is so analysed.

The person is first analysed under two categories: *Nāma* and *Rūpa*. *Nāma* (literally Name), is usually translated into English by the word 'Mind', but in Buddhist psychology it is used as a collective name to refer to the psychological and mental aspects of the human being. *Rūpa* (literally Form), translated into English by the word ('Matter', 'Body' or 'Corporeality'), is also a collective term to describe the physical aspect of being. Thus *Nāmarūpa* (Name and Form) taken together comprise the psycho-physical organism which constitutes a person as a separate and distinct individual.

It is extremely important to stress that Buddhism does not think of *Nāma* and *Rūpa* in dualistic terms. They are inter-dependent and belong to each other in an integral manner. One cannot exist without the other. As Buddhaghosa has put it: 'Form (*rūpa*) goes on when supported by Name (*nāma*), and Name when supported by Form.'[2]

He further illustrates this relationship by likening *Nāma* and *Rūpa* to a blind man and to a cripple, who are helpless when separate, but can support one another if they agree to work together; the lame man mounting the blind man and directing the way, while the latter carries him on the way.[3]

The same idea is expressed in the following verses:

> As a pair are mind and body both
> To one another a support;
> As soon as one of them dissolves,
> The other too does disappear. . . .
>
> As men are able with a ship
> To cross the waters of the sea,
> Just so, supported by this body,
> The mind keeps going on and on.
>
> And just as with the help of men
> The ship may cross the mighty sea,
> Just so supported by the mind
> The body may be keeping on.
>
> As men and ship traverse the sea,
> Depending on each other's help,
> So are the mind and body too,
> Each other they support and help.[4]

There is much in common between the Buddhist view of the relationship between Mind and Matter and the view held by some process thinkers such as Sewell Wright, whose view is expressed in the following passage:

> If mind and matter are coextensive, they may be looked upon as two aspects of the same reality. They do not, however, stand on an equal footing. All that any of us can know directly is our own memories, emotions, thoughts and volitions. Matter (or physical action) is always a deduction from regularities that we find in our experience. In general, mind may be considered the inner aspect of the reality of the observer, matter the external aspect of a reality in the inner aspect of which the observer does not partake, except in so far as perception implies interaction.[5]

But unlike modern process philosophy, which recognises an inner reality called by some 'the within of things' (Teilhard de Chardin) or the 'element of mind' (Hartshorne), Buddhism does not accept any such permanent element; even the mind is regarded as unstable and in perpetual flux. As Buddhaghosa says:

> . . . this that we call mind, that we call consciousness, arises as one thing, ceases as another; whether by day or by night. Just as a monkey faring through the woods, through the great forests, catches hold of one bough, letting it go, seizes another; even so that which we call mind, consciousness, that arises as one thing, ceases as another, both by day and night.[6]

In fact the body can be regarded as more stable than the mind. Perhaps the insistence that the mind is less stable than the bodily substance was to leave no room at all for identifying the *ātman* with any aspect of the mind, which is more likely than identifying it with the body. This is the implication of the following passage:

> It would be better for an untaught ordinary man to treat as self (*attā*) this body, which is constructed upon the four great primaries of matter (*mahā-bhūta*), than mind. Why? Because the body can last one year, two years . . . even a hundred years; but what is called 'mind' and 'thinking' and 'consciousness' arises and ceases differently through night and day.[7]

Another passage affirms emphatically that consciousness is *anattā*.

> Consciousness is not-self. Also the causes and conditions of the arising of consciousness, they like-wise are not-self. Hence, how could it be possible that consciousness having arisen through something which is not-self, could ever be a self?[8]

(b) Pañcakkhandha analysis

The division of man into the two categories, *Nāma* and *Rūpa*, is only the first step in the Buddhist analysis of the self. The next step is the analysis of man into the five *khandhas* (aggregates). This is the classic Theravāda *Pañcakkhandha* theory, according to which the individual consists of 1. *Rūpa* 2. *Vedanā* 3. *Saññā* 4. *Saṃkhāra* and 5. *Viññāna*. The last four are sub-divisions of *Nāma*. These five aggregates have been the subject of minute psychological studies

especially in the *Abhidhamma*. The following is a brief description of
the five aggregates.

  i. *Rūpa* (matter). It is sense data without substance. It consists of
     four primary elements (a) *Paṭhavī* (earth), i.e. solidity,
     hardness, rigidity or compactness of matter; (b) *Āpo* (water),
     i.e. liquidity, viscidity or cohesion; (c) *Tejo* (fire), i.e. heat
     and cold, and all degrees of temperature; (d) *Vāyo* (air), i.e.
     distension and motion. It represents the more restless and
     dynamic aspects of matter.
 ii. *Vēdanā* (sensation or feeling) consisting of the six organs of
     sense, viz. sight, hearing, smell, touch, taste and mind
     (*manas*).
iii. *Saññā* (perceptions). The faculty that receives impressions of
     objects whether physical or mental. They are of six kinds:
     impression of colour and shape, sound, odour, taste, touch-
     able things, non-mental objects.
 iv. *Saṃkhārā* (mental states or activities, volition). Fifty mental
     activities are mentioned. This word has a wide range of
     meanings and there is no proper English equivalent which
     gives the exact connotation of the Pali term.
  v. *Viññāṇa* (consciousness), i.e. reaction or response which has
     one of the six faculties as its basis, and one of the six external
     phenomena as its object. Consciousness is said to be pure
     sensation, without any content. It must not be confused with
     what western thinkers call mind, which is active. Therefore,
     consciousness never arises alone, but must always be sup-
     ported by the elements, one of the senses and an object of
     sense. Thus visual consciousness is made up of pure con-
     sciousness, together with the sense of vision, an object of
     vision and some colour or shape. Consciousness is further
     defined as 'awareness', in every single case of what is now
     present to the senses, or to the mind. Consciousness appears
     to be like a mirror which simply reflects whatever is brought
     in front of it.

Briefly, we might say that the psychosomatic organism consists of a
compound of material stuff (*rūpa*) and emotional, conative, vol-
itional and cognitive faculties of the mind (*nāma*).

Altogether there are eighty-one basic elements with the addition
of the element of space (*Ākāso*), which is counted as one of the *rūpa*

elements. None of these elements is permanent. Hence there is no soul. When the five aggregates come together they take a certain form or shape and what is thus formed is given a name. Thus we have 'name and form' (*nāma-rūpa*), but when the elements disintegrate there is no *nāma-rūpa*, no person, no ego.

Regarding the impersonality and emptiness (*suññatā*) of the five aggregates it is said:

> Whatever there is of corporeality, feeling, perception, mental formations and consciousness, whether past, present or future, one's own or external, gross or subtle, lofty or low, far or near, this one should understand according to reality and true wisdom: 'This does not belong to me. This I am not, this is not my Ego.'[9]

In another passage the same idea is expressed more forcefully:

> Suppose that a man who is not blind were to behold the many bubbles on the Ganges as they are driving along, and should watch them and carefully examine them. After carefully examining them, however, they will appear to him empty, unreal and unsubstantial. In exactly the same way does the monk behold all the corporeal phenomena . . . feelings . . . perceptions . . . mental formations . . . states of consciousness, whether they be of the past, present or future . . . far or near. And he watches them and examines them carefully: and after carefully examining them they appear to him empty, unreal and unsubstantial.[10]

The famous chariot illustration in the conversations of the Arahant Nāgasena and King Milinda, elucidates the significance of the *Pañcakkhandhā* theory, and the passage where this occurs deserves to be quoted rather fully:

> Milinda, the King, spoke to the venerable Nāgasena as follows: 'How is your reverence called? Bhante, what is your name?'
>
> 'Your majesty, I am called Nāgasena; my fellow priests, your majesty, address me as Nāgasena: but whether parents give one the name Nāgasena, or Sūrasena, or Vīrasena, or Sinhasena, it is, nevertheless, your majesty, but a way of counting, a term, an appellation, a convenient designation, a mere name, this Nāgasena; for there is no Ego (*atta*) to be found here.'

Then said Milinda, the King:

'Listen to me, Lords, . . . Nāgasena here says thus, "There is no Ego to be found here." Is it possible, pray, for me to assent to what he says?'

And Milinda, the King, spoke to the venerable Nāgasena thus:

'Bhante Nāgasena, if there is no Ego to be found, who is it then furnishes you priests with the priestly requisites, robes, . . . in that case there is no merit, there is no demerit, there is no one who does, or causes to be done, meritorious or demeritorious deeds, neither good nor evil deeds can have any fruit or result. Bhante Nāgasena, neither is he a murderer who kills a priest, nor can you priests have any teacher, preceptor, or ordination. When you say, "My fellow-priests, your majesty, address me as Nāgasena", what then is this Nāgasena?'

'Pray, Bhante, is the hair of the head Nāgasena?'

'Nay, verily, your majesty.'

'Is the hair of the body Nāgasena?'

'Nay, verily, your majesty.'

'Are then, Bhante, form, sensation, perception, the pre-dispositions, and consciousness, unitedly, Nāgasena?'

'Nay, verily, your majesty.'

'Is it then, Bhante, something besides form, sensation . . . consciousness, which is Nāgasena?'

'Nay, verily, your majesty.'

'Bhante, although I question you very closely, I fail to discover any Nāgasena. Verily now, Bhante, Nāgasena is an empty sound. What Nāgasena is there here? Bhante, you speak a lie, a falsehood. There is no Nāgasena.'

Then the venerable Nāgasena spoke to the King as follows:

'Your majesty, you are a delicate prince, an exceedingly delicate prince, and if, your majesty, you walk in the middle of the day on hot, sandy, ground, . . . your feet become sore, your body tired, the mind oppressed, and the body-consciousness suffers. Pray, did you come afoot or riding?'

'Bhante, I do not go afoot, I came in a chariot.'

'Your majesty, if you came in a chariot, declare to me the chariot. Pray, your majesty, is the pole the chariot?

'Nay, verily, Bhante.'

'Is the axle the chariot?'

'Nay, verily, Bhante.'

'Is the chariot-wheel, the banner-staff, . . . the chariot?'

'Nay, verily, Bhante.'

'Is it then something else besides pole, wheels, . . . which is the chariot?'

'Nay, verily, Bhante.'

'Your majesty, though I question you very closely, I fail to discover any chariot. Verily now, your majesty, the word chariot is an empty sound: what chariot is there here? Your majesty, you speak a falsehood, a lie. There is no chariot here. . . . Listen to me, my Lords, Milinda the king says thus, "I came in a chariot", and being requested, "Your majesty, if you came in a chariot, declare to me the chariot," he fails to produce the chariot. Is it possible, pray, for me to assent to what he says?'

'. . . Bhante Nāgasena, I speak no lie: the word "chariot" is but a way of counting, term, appellation, convenient designation, and name for pole, axle, chariot-body, and banner-staff.' 'Thoroughly well, your majesty, do you understand a chariot. In exactly the same way, your majesty, in respect of me, Nāgasena is but a way of counting, . . . for the hair of my head, form, sensation, . . . consciousness. But in the absolute sense there is no Ego [*attā*] to be found. And the priestess Vajirā said as follows in the presence of the blessed One.

> Even as the word of 'chariot' means
> That members join to frame a whole
> So when the groups [*khandhas*] appear to view,
> We use the phrase a living-being.[11]

This conversation is considered to give expression to the Theravāda view that the individual is a combination of five aggregates with no permanent identifiable entity; the notion of the self as an entity, is the result of the mistaken identification of one of the aggregates with the so-called self. This is a point that is stressed over and over again. Thus:

When one says 'I', what one does is that one refers to all the *khandhas* combined or to any one of them, and deludes oneself that that was 'I'. Just as one cannot say that the fragrance of the lotus belonged to the petals, the colour or the pollen, so one could not say that the *rūpa* was 'I' or the *vedanā* was 'I' or any other of the *khandhas* was 'I'. There is nowhere to be found in the *khandhas* 'I am'.[12]

In the *Kathāvatthu* practically all possible questions regarding the existence of the person (*puggala*) are asked, and in every instance the reality of the *puggala* is denied. *Puggala* is here explained by *atta* (self, ego, personal entity) *satta* (being) and *jīva* (vital principle, soul etc.). *Puggala* therefore covers all that 'person' or 'personality' means, and the different terms used to designate the *puggala* have a validity only in a relative sense, namely in figures of speech, popular designations and expressions in conventional language (*vohāra*), but not in an absolute sense (*paramattha*). Thus, wherever in the texts mention is made of a person, a self, or rebirth of a being, they should be understood as a mere 'conventional mode of speech' (*vohāravacana*), and not in the absolute or ultimate sense (*paramattha*). The only actual realities are those psycho-physical phenomena, although they have only a momentary duration. There is no permanent reality; the only reality is impermanence.

2.   THE ETHICAL ARGUMENT

The ethical argument briefly is that the delusion of a permanent self is the root cause of *dukkha* and so one must get rid of the false notion of the self by traversing the Noble Eightfold Path. It is the false notion of the self that gives rise to *taṇhā* (craving), which in turn leads to birth, decay, old age and death (*jāti, jarā, maraṇa*). As long as there is a belief in the existence of the 'self', there will be thirst for existence, and as long as there is a craving for existence there will be a manifestation of the *khandhas* in some concrete form, which is subject to *dukkha*. This is stated in two passages in the Saṃyutta Nikāya as follows:

> The arising, presence and manifestation of materiality, feeling, perception, formations and consciousness, is but the arising of suffering, the presence of maladies, the manifestation of decay and death.[13]

Therefore,

> Whoso delights in materiality, in feeling, in perception, in

formations and consciousness, he delights in suffering; and whoso delights in suffering will not be freed from suffering.[14]

Walpola Rāhula, expressing the Theravāda point of view, traces all the evils in the world to this erroneous view of the self:

> Buddhism stands unique in the history of human thought in denying the existence of such a Soul, Self, or Ātman. According to the teaching of the Buddha, the idea of self is an imaginary, false belief which has no corresponding reality, and it produces harmful thoughts of 'me' and 'mine', selfish desire, craving, attachment, hatred, ill-will, conceit, pride, egoism, and other defilements, impurities and problems. It is the source of all the troubles in the world from personal conflicts to wars between nations. In short, to this false view can be traced all the evil in the world.[15]

If, as Rāhula says, all the evils in the world, all suffering, can be traced to the false notion of the self, then logically it follows that in order to be free from *dukkha* one must attain to the knowledge that in reality there is no self.

In the *Anattalakkhaṇa Sutta* the analytical and the ethical arguments are correlated. The five aggregates of the psycho-physical complex are analysed in the way stated above and are shown to be devoid of any soul substance. In this way the conclusion is reached that all things, past, future or present, in oneself or external, gross or subtle, inferior or superior, far or near, must be viewed thus: 'This is not mine, this is not what I am, this is not myself' (*na me so attā*). It is then added, that when one realises this truth of *anattā* and holds no theory (*diṭṭhi*) about the self, one can by spiritual discipline eradicate desire (*taṇhā*) and attain the goal of release.

Three steps are noticeable in the argument of the *Anattalakkhaṇa Sutta*.

Firstly, if there is an immortal soul it could not be subject to suffering:

> The body (*rūpa*), O bhikkhus, is soulless (*anattā*). If, O bhikkhus, there were in this a soul, then this body would not be subject to suffering. 'Let this body be thus, let this body be not thus,' such possibilities would also exist. But inasmuch as this

body is soulless, it is subject to suffering, and no possibility exists for [ordering]: 'Let this be so, let this be not so.'[16]

In like manner the other four *khandhas* are taken in turn and the same argument is applied to them.

Secondly, if all the *khandhas* are subject to suffering it means that they are impermanent, and if so there can be no permanent entity about which one can say, 'this is my soul.'

'What think ye, O bhikkhus, is this body permanent or impermanent?'
'Impermanent [*anicca*], Lord.'
'Is that which is impermanent happy or painful?'
'It is painful [*dukkha*], Lord.'
'Is it justifiable, then, to think of that which is impermanent, painful and transitory: "This is mine; this am I; this is my soul?"'
'Certainly not, Lord.'[17]

The same argument is repeated in respect of the other *khandhas*.

The ethical import of the first two arguments is drawn in the third step. If all the *khandhas* are subject to *dukkha* and *anicca*, one should by right knowledge understand their real nature. When the true nature of all things is perceived, one conceives an aversion to them and becomes divested of passion (*taṇhā*) and by the absence of passion one becomes free.

Then, O Bhikkhus, all body, whether past, present or future, personal or external, coarse or subtle, low or high, far or near, should be understood by right knowledge in its real nature – 'This is not mine; this am I not; this is not my soul.'
All feelings, perceptions, mental states and consciousness, whether past, present or future, personal or external, coarse or subtle, low or high, far or near, should be understood by right knowledge in their real nature as: 'These are not mine; these am I not; these are not my soul.'
The learned Aryan disciple who sees thus gets a disgust for body, for feelings, for perceptions, for mental states, for consciousness, is detached from the abhorrent thing and is emancipated through detachment. Then dawns on him the knowledge – 'Emancipated am I'. He understands that rebirth is ended, lived

is the Holy Life, done what should be done, there is no more of this state again.'[18]

3. RELATION TO ANICCA AND DUKKHA

The relation of *anattā* to *anicca* and *dukkha* is implied in the above quotations from the *Anattalakkhaṇa Sutta*. The fact of *anattā* is corroborated by the fact of *anicca*, which, by stressing the transient character of all *khandhas*, leaves absolutely no room for any notion of a permanent self or substance.

Throughout his life, the Buddha constantly reminded his disciples of the transitoriness (*anicca*) of all phenomena, by repeating the classic statement: *Aniccā vata saṃkhārā uppādavayadhammino* (impermanent are the *saṃkhārā* which are subject to origin and decay). This, as well as the oft-recurrent formula: *sabbe saṃkhārā aniccā*[19] (all *saṃkhārā* are impermanent), is on the lips of every Buddhist in Sri Lanka. Both these expressions stress that all conditioned things or phenomenal processess, mental as well as material, are impermanent or transient and subject to arising and passing away. The last words that the Buddha said just before he passed away were also a reminder of this truth, which one should take to heart, diligently seeking to be delivered from conditioned existence. He said: '*Vayadhammā saṃkhārā, appamādena sampādetha*' (Subject to decay are all compounded things. Do ye abide in heedfulness).[20]

Anicca is an empirically observable fact. That all things rise, decay and fall is an objectively evident everyday occurrence.[21] This characteristic of the inconsistency of things extends even to the periodical destruction of the world-systems.[22] What is important is for one to realise that one is also subject to the same law that governs all external things. Thus:

It would be better for an untaught ordinary man to treat as self [*attā*] this body, which is constructed upon the four great elements [*mahābhūta*], than cognisance [*citta*]. Why? Because this body can last one year, two years . . . even a hundred years; but what is called cognisance [*citta*] and mind [*mano*] and consciousness [*viññāṇa*] arises and ceases differently through night and day, just as a monkey ranging through a forest seizes a branch, and, letting that go, seizes another.[23]

The importance of the Buddhist analysis of matter, which includes the primary elements (*mahābhūtas*) and the secondary elements (*uppādā-rūpas*) is to leave no room whatsoever for a notion of the self. Without the realisation that 'decay is inherent in all things,' that insight that the notion of selfhood and the idea of change are inseparable, there can be no deliverance from saṃsāric existence. To drive home this fact the Buddha once took a small piece of cowdung in his hand and told a Bhikkhu:

> There is no materiality whatever, O monks, no feeling, no perception, no formations, no consciousness whatever that is permanent, everlasting, eternal, changeless, identically abiding for ever. — Then the Blessed One took a bit of cowdung in his hand and he spoke to the monks: 'Monks, if even that much of permanent, everlasting, eternal, changeless individual selfhood [*attabhāva*], identically abiding for ever, could be found, then this living of a life of purity [*brahmacariya*] for the complete eradication of Ill [*dukkhakkhaya*] would not be feasible.'[24]

This passage clearly shows that *anattā* and *anicca* are no theoretical matters but have a direct bearing on *dukkha*. The three go together. One can be understood only in relation to the other two. *Dukkha* is a word that has varied shades of meaning and defies precise definition. The word suffering is often used for *dukkha* but is not an adequate term. There is no one word in English that can cover the wide range of meanings as *dukkha* in Pali. Such terms as discomfort, illness, unsatisfactoriness, unrest, anxiety, state of commotion, conflict and existential anxiety are used in different contexts to express the meaning of *dukkha*. It is a word that describes the predicament in which man is, bound by conditioned existence in saṃsāric life. It is *taṇhā*, the desire or thirst to exist, to re-exist, to continue to exist, which arises as a result of the belief in a permanent self or soul which has thrown man into the predicament in which he is. Therefore to eliminate *dukkha* one has to eliminate the root cause of *dukkha*, namely, *taṇhā*, which in effect means the elimination of the notion of the self. For this it is necessary that one comes to a true understanding of the real nature of the self – that is that there is no permanent self; that one is *anattā*. Thus we may state the relevance of the *anattā* doctrine to the human predicament as follows.

Man is in this *dukkha* predicament because of his attachment (*taṇhā*), to a false notion of the self conceived as a permanent entity.

In this predicament in which man is threatened by the possibility of non-being, he seeks for some security and imagines that he has an immortal 'soul' on which he can depend. But he cannot escape the fact that 'decay is inherent in all things.' This fact comes into conflict with his imaginary notion of the self. This conflict is the cause of *dukkha*; it is the state of existential anxiety. It is an imaginary state of conflict between the real (i.e. the actual fact of universal decay or *anicca*) and the unreal conceptual invention of a permanent immortal 'self'. This is an ideological conflict, a conflict between the fact of impermanence and the false notion of a permanent 'self'. And the solution to the problem consists in dispelling the false notion of the 'self'. When it is seen that decay (*anicca*) is inherent even in the so-called self, when one realises that even the so-called self is impermanent, the conflict ceases and *dukkha* comes to an end, for there can be no conflict between the law of impermanence (*anicca*) and the impermanent self (*anattā*), because they are seen to be identical. Hence, it is of the utmost importance for one to realise the fact of soullessness (*anattā*). It is this realisation that leads to freedom from *dukkha*. The sole purpose of the minute analysis of the empirical self is to bring man to this realisation.

4 The Theravāda Point of View

1. NEITHER ETERNALISM NOR NIHILISM

The denial of the *ātman* of an unchanging, undying essence, does not mean that the Buddha held a nihilistic view of the total annihilation of body and mind with the extinction of *taṇhā*. That the Buddha held no extreme view – either an eternalist view or an annihilationist view – is clearly stated in the texts.

The fourth book of the *Abhidhamma* states that there are three types of teachers in the world. Firstly, the one who teaches that there is no soul or self at all; that whatever there is, is temporal and perishable. He is called a nihilist or an annihilationist (*uccheda vādin*). Secondly, there is the one who teaches that the soul is immortal and imperishable. He is called an eternalist (*sassata vādin*). Thirdly, there is one who teaches neither. He is the Buddha. He is neither an eternalist nor a nihilist.[1]

This idea is expressed figuratively in the *Dhammapada*, where eternalism and nihilism are likened to two warrior kings, who are to be conquered if the goal is to be reached:

> Having killed mother (craving), father (conceit), two warrior kings (eternalism and nihilism), and having destroyed a country (sense-avenues and sense-objects) together with its revenue officer (attachment), ungrieving goes the Brahmin (the Arahant).[2]

The *Dhammasaṅganī* dismisses both eternalism and nihilism as speculative theories:

> What is that sort of speculation known as Eternalism? That both soul and world are eternal etc.
> What is that sort of speculation known as Annihilation? That both soul and world will be dissolved . . .

All this sort of opinion, walking in opinion, jungle of opinion, wilderness of opinion . . . the grip and tenacity of it, the inclination towards it . . . this stiffness of grasp – this is what is called speculative opinion.[3]

That the Buddha avoided the extreme of eternalism and nihilism is clearly seen in his conversation with Vacchagotta, who pressed the Buddha for a direct answer to the question: Is there a self or is there not a self?

The wanderer, Vacchagotta, spoke thus to the Lord: Now, good Gotama, is there a Self? When he had spoken thus the Lord became silent.

What, then, good Gotama, is there not a Self? And a second time the Lord became silent. Then the wanderer, Vacchagotta, rising from his seat, departed. Then soon after his departure the venerable Ānanda spoke thus to the Lord:

Why, Lord, did not the Lord answer Vacchagotta the wanderer's question?

If I, Ānanda, on being asked by the wanderer Vacchagotta, if there is a Self, should have answered that there is a Self, this, Ānanda, would have been a siding-in with those recluses and Brāhmaṇas who are Eternalists. If I, Ānanda, on being asked by the wanderer, Vacchagotta, if there is not a Self, should have answered that there is not a Self, this Ānanda, would have been a siding-in with those recluses and Brāhmaṇas who are Annihilationists.

If I, Ānanda, on being asked by the wanderer, Vacchagotta, if there is a Self, should have answered that there is a Self, would this have been in accordance with my knowledge that 'all things are not Self'?

This would have not been so, Lord.

If, Ānanda, I, on being asked by the wanderer, Vacchagotta, if there is not a Self, should have answered that there is not a Self, the wanderer Vacchagotta, already confused, would have been increasingly confused and he would have thought: Was there not formerly a Self for me? There is none now.[4]

The Buddha makes it clear that he was silent when Vacchagotta put the question to him because he did not want to side in with the eternalists or nihilists, for both these views are not in keeping with his knowledge that 'all things are not-self'.

It is quite clear that in this context *anattā* means neither an absolute negation, nor a positive affirmation. Walpola Rāhula states the Theravāda position thus:

> According to the Buddha's teaching, it is as wrong to hold the opinion, 'I have no self' (which is the annihilationist theory) as to hold the opinion 'I have self' (which is the eternalist theory) because both are fetters, both arising out of the false idea 'I am'. The correct position with regard to the question of *anattā* is not to take hold of any opinions or views, but to try to see things objectively as they are, without mental projections, to see that what I call 'I' or 'being' is only a combination of physical and mental aggregates, which are working together inter-dependently in a flux of momentary change within the law of cause and effect, and that there is nothing permanent, everlasting, unchanging and eternal in the whole of existence.[5]

The correct position, as Rāhula says, is to look at things objectively and see their real nature as a combination of psycho-physical aggregates in a continuous process of change. In other words one must come to a knowledge of the fact that all is *anicca*. Such knowledge will dispel any erroneous notion of a permanent, self-existing 'I'.

2.   ETHICO-RELIGIOUS MOTIVATION

For a proper evaluation of the Buddhist view of finitude, it is of fundamental importance to understand clearly that the elaborate meticulous analysis of the nature of conditioned existence is undertaken in Buddhism, not for its own sake, but in order to provide a motivation for ethical conduct that would lead to salvation from the human predicament. This is a point we have drawn attention to and needs to be stressed even at the risk of repetition. Y. Karunadasa explains the ethico-religious motivation as follows:

> The exact nature of the earliest form of Buddhism is still a matter of controversy. However, on the basis of the Pali Nikāyas

as they exist in their present form it may be said that Buddhism is, in the main, a doctrine of salvation. Deliverance from the 'Saṃsāric' plane of existence, in other words, the realization of *Nibbāna*, is its final goal. Its analysis of the world of experience is undertaken, not for its own sake, but for evolving a rationale for its practical doctrine and discipline. Attention is not concentrated on the empirical world in and for itself. The Buddhist inquiry into the nature and constitution of matter and its relevance to Buddhism as a spiritual discipline cannot be properly understood if the subject is divorced from this religious context.[6]

One of the oft-repeated statements, namely '*rūpam sañyojanīyo dhammo*'[7] (i.e. matter is something that is conducive to or productive of fetters) indicates the relation between the Buddhist analysis of matter and ethical conduct. *Rūpa* or matter is not a fetter in itself. It is the *upādāna*, 'the laying hold of' or craving for *rūpa* that constitutes the fetter. Hence the need to understand and comprehend (*pariññeyya*) the nature of *rūpa* as impermanent (*anicca*), which therefore cannot be made the basis of true happiness, so that one may through ethical discipline eradicate all desire for conditioned existence. The elaborate analysis of existence is thus undertaken, as Karunadasa says, in the interest of ethical discipline that would lead to salvation from *saṃsāra*. The deep ethical commitment in Buddhism is directed to this end – to deliverance from conditioned existence which is subject to *dukkha*.

The emphasis on ethical commitment is all the more weighty because according to Buddhism one finds deliverance within oneself alone. One must therefore work out one's own salvation by one's efforts, without depending on any external power. The Buddha is represented as saying:

> Verily I declare to you, my friend, that within this very body, mortal as it is and only a fathom high, but conscious and endowed with mind, is the world and the waxing thereof and the waning thereof and the way that leads to the passing away thereof.[8]

Commenting on this passage A. B. Keith says:

> ... the statement, in fact, is not intended to be a deliverance from metaphysics; it is merely an assertion of the simple truth, from the Buddhist point of view, that the essential fact of existence

is the misery which affects the individual and from which it is the individual who, by his own effort in following the true path of salvation, must work out his own destiny.[9]

This means that the malady and the remedy lie within man himself. Man is responsible for the predicament in which he is, and the whole responsibility of deliverance is his alone. Buddhist soteriology is therefore anthropocentric or homocentric. Hence Buddhism is not interested in metaphysics; it is interested in ethics.

The ethical significance of *anicca* and its bearing on *dukkha* and *anattā* are brought out in a number of passages. In the *Mahāvagga* the Buddha admonishes his disciples thus:

> Impermanent, Brethren, are [all] *Saṃkhāras*, unstable [not constant], Brethren, are [all] *Saṃkhāras*, [hence] not a cause of comfort and satisfaction are [all] *Saṃkhāras*, so much so that one must get tired of all these *Saṃkhāras*, be disgusted with them, and be completely free of them.[10]

In another passage the Buddha, indicating the all-inclusive character of the *Saṃkhāras*, says:

> There will come a time, Brethren, maybe hundreds of thousands of years hence, when no more rains will fall, and consequently all plants and trees, all vegetation, will dry up and be destroyed; with the scorching due to the appearance of a second sun, streams and rivulets will go dry; and with the appearance of a third, such large rivers as the Ganges and Jamuna will dry up; similarly, the lakes and even the great ocean itself will dry up in course of time, and even such great mountains as the Sineru, nay even this wide earth, will begin to smoke and be burnt up in a great and universal holocaust. . . . Thus impermanent, Brethren, are all *Saṃkhāras*, unstable, and hardly a cause for comfort, so much so that one (contemplating their impermanent nature) must necessarily get tired of them.[11]

The ethical significance of the law of *anicca* is well brought out in another passage where the Buddha tells Ānanda about the glories of the famous king Mahā Sudassana – about his cities, treasures, palaces and all other luxurious possessions, which came to naught at his death – and drew the moral lesson:

Behold, Ananda, how all these things (*Saṃkhārā*) are now dead and gone, have passed and vanished away. Thus, impermanent, Ānanda, are the *Saṃkhāras*: thus untrustworthy, Ānanda, are the *Saṃkhāras*. And this, Ānanda, is enough to be weary of, to be disgusted with and be completely free of, such *Saṃkhāras*.[12]

It is by the contemplation of impermanence (*aniccānupassanā*) that one develops insight and becomes free from the three-fold clinging – i.e. clinging to views (*diṭṭhūpādāna*), clinging to mere rules and rituals (*sīlabbataparāmāsa*), and clinging to personality belief (*attavādūpādāna*). One thus becomes a faith-devotee (*saddhānusārī*) and reaches the stage of perfection when one is called a *saddhāvimutta* (faith-liberated).

In him who considers all formations as impermanent, conditionless deliverance [*animittavimokkha*] is predominant; therefore, he too is called faith-liberated.[13]

In the *Anicca Sutta*, the Buddha enumerates seven gift-worthy persons who see impermanency in all compounded things and thereby are liberated from the law of *anicca*.[14] To be free from the law of *anicca* is to be liberated from *dukkha*. The perception that all things are *anicca* leads to the perception that all is *dukkha* and to the realisation of the truth of *anattā*, which frees man from the predicament in which he is.

3. THE EXISTENTIAL SIGNIFICANCE

It is important to note that the doctrine of *anattā* arose, not from a theoretical interest – empirical, psychological or biological – but from an existential concern. It arose out of Prince Siddhārtha's experience when he saw the three sights – an old man, a sick man and a corpse – which is vividly described in traditional accounts.[15] There is a striking parallel in Nietzsche's *Zarathustra* in the chapter 'The Preacher of Death', in which he refers to three ways in which the threat of non-being comes to man: 'They meet an invalid, or an old man or a corpse, and immediately say "life is refuted".'[16] However, Nietzsche speaks of a 'courage' which can affirm life in the midst of the threat to life. Through his experience Prince Siddhārtha also discovered a moral force by which the threat to life could be met.

Three things happened to Prince Siddhārtha when he saw these three sights. Firstly, he realised the universal nature of all existence, the fact that all living beings are subject to decay and death. Secondly, he applied this to himself and came to the realisation that he too is subject to decay and death – 'life is refuted'. But thirdly, this realisation drove him to seek for a rationale of authentic living, by which the threat to life could be met. Again there is a parallel here between Siddhārtha's thought and Nietzsche's philosophy of life.

According to Paul Tillich, 'Nietzsche is the most impressive and effective representative of what could be called a "philosophy of life",[17] the principle of which is 'the will power'. By this he means the power that preserves and enhances life amidst the struggle for survival, and therefore runs through all existence. 'It is a principle whereby man consciously orders the available possibilities of his environment, and to reach this sort of mastery one must be disciplined, must first of all master himself and his own capacities.'[18] The Buddha also spoke of self-mastery as the key to life, for which a strict discipline is necessary. The drive to such a self-mastery arises when man realises the fact that he is mortal.

We could relate this to what the father of modern existentialism, Søren Kierkegaard, said. He pointed out that a man who comes to realise that 'all men are mortal' knows the universal essence of all existence, but what is needed is that he should apply this truth to himself and come to the conclusion in his own case, 'I too must die'. It is then that an individual will feel the need to find a purpose, a plan and a destiny in life. Kierkegaard's aim was to help men to come to that conclusion and thus experience the truth – one might say the truth of *anicca*, *dukkha* and *anattā* – in their own individual existence so that they will seek for a rationale for true living. From this existential point of view the doctrine of *anattā* has a deep significance in biblical theology and it is in this context that the psycho-physical analysis of existence becomes meaningful.

5 The Problem of Self-identity

I. ANATTĀ AND REBIRTH

One of the haunting problems that has dogged Theravāda Buddhism from very early times is to reconcile the doctrine of *anattā* with the belief in *karma* and rebirth. T. W. Rhys Davids, pointing out that the Buddha was led into an untenable situation by, on the one hand, preaching the doctrine of *anattā* and, on the other hand, accepting the belief in rebirth, says:

> We have thus arrived at a deadlock: to save what it holds to be a psychological truth Buddhism rejects the notion of a soul; to save what it holds to be the necessity of justice, it retains the belief in transmigration.[1]

The word transmigration is misleading. The Buddhist belief in rebirth or rather rebecoming must be distinguished from the Hindu belief in a transmigrating soul. (I do not mean that Rhys Davids was not aware of this distinction or that he did not know what the Buddhist belief was.) What rebirth meant in the Buddhist context therefore needs some explanation. The Buddhist teaching is that *taṇhā* (thirst, desire, craving), which manifests itself in various ways, is that which gives rise to rebirth. It is the will to live, to exist, to re-exist; it is clinging to existence, striving for existence by way of good or bad actions (*Kusalākusalakamma*). There is no end to the stream of becoming as long as *karma* persists.

The term *karma* (Pali *Kamma*), literally means action or deed, and the Law of *karma* is the law of cause and effect, the logical consequence of deeds. Good actions produce good results, and bad actions produce bad results. This law of cause and effect or action and reaction is expressed in the two opening verses of the *Dhammapada*:

Karma

All that we are is the result of what we have thought; it is founded on our thoughts, it is made up of our thoughts. If a man speaks or acts with an evil thought, pain follows him, as the wheel follows the foot of the ox that draws the cart. . . . If a man speaks or acts with a pure thought, happiness follows, like a shadow that never leaves him.[2]

The verses from the *Dhammapada* emphasise the initial importance of thought or mind (*mano*), as producing the good or bad effects. Other passages in the *Piṭakas* emphasise this and that still prior factor of the will in the thinker, speaker and doer:

It is the custom for a *Tathāgata* (Truth-finder) to lay down 'Deed, deed'. I lay down three kinds of deeds for the doing of an evil deed: deed of body, deed of speech, deed of mind. Of these kinds of deeds thus classified, I lay down that a deed of mind is the most greatly censurable in the doing of an evil deed.

I, monks, say that willing is a deed. Having willed, one does a deed, through body, speech or thought. . . . The fruit of a deed is threefold, it may arise here and now, or later, or in a succession of lives.[3]

The Law of *karma* operates in its own field without the intervention of an external ruling agency or lawgiver. It is a law in itself. Within *karma* itself is the potentiality of producing its due effect. The cause produces the effect; the effect explains the cause, just as the seed produces the fruit and the fruit explains the seed. Both are interrelated. Even so is *karma*.

As long as this karmic force survives, there is rebirth or rebecoming. This process of rebecoming is fully explained in the theory of Dependent Origination, or Conditioned Co-production (*Paṭicca-samuppāda*). The principle of this theory is given in a short formula of four lines: 'When this is, that is: this arising, that arises; when this is not, that is not; this ceasing, that ceases.' The traditional explanation of this doctrine is that it is concerned only with the process of birth and death; it deals with the cause of rebirth and suffering and is not a theory of evolution or of the origin of life.

If, on account of a cause, an effect comes to be, then if the cause ceases, the effect also must cease. The complete cessation of ignorance leads to the cessation of birth and death. This process of cause and effect continues *ad infinitum*. The beginning of this process cannot be determined, as it is impossible to say whence this life-flux was encompassed by ignorance. But when ignorance is dispelled by knowledge and the life-flux is transmuted into *Nirvāna* then the end of the cycle of birth and death, of *Saṃsāra*, comes about.

2. THE STATES OF EXISTENCE

As long as the process of life continues as a result of *karma*, a being will be born in various states in accordance with his good or bad deeds. In one of the Suttas there is a reference to five states of existence. They are as follows: (1) the lower worlds (*duggati*, *vinipāta*, *niraya*); (2) the animal kingdom (*tiracchānayoni*); (3) the spirit-sphere (*pettivisaya*) or sphere of ghost-beings and demons; (4) realm of human beings (*manussā*); and (5) realm of gods (*devaloka*) and higher beings or spirits. The highest realm is known as the Formless realm (*arūpaloka*) where the spirits have no bodily form. These spheres of existence are subdivided into a number of stages or states, numbering thirty-one.

The five states of existence are graded according to the amount or degrees of pain or suffering experienced in them. The experience in the 'lower worlds' is said to be extremely unpleasant. In the animal sphere it is unpleasant, since animals are supposed to live in a state of constant fear with strong unsatisfied instinctive desires such as hunger and thirst. In the spirit-sphere it is more unpleasant than pleasant. In the human world there are more pleasant than unpleasant experiences. In the deva-worlds the experience is extremely pleasant. The age of a being in the highest formless realm is said to be 84,000 *Mahā-kappas* (Great Aeons).

The lower worlds are compared to a pit of coals into which one falls; animal existence is a pit full of excrement; existence in the spirit-sphere is like coming under a tree in a desert without much shade; human life is compared to coming under a shady tree, while the deva-world is compared to a well-furnished and beautiful palace.

3. HOW REBIRTH TAKES PLACE

Nyānatiloka Mahāthera explains the Theravāda view of Rebirth as follows:

According to Buddhism, there are three factors necessary for the rebirth of a human being, that is, for the formation of the embryo in the mother's womb. They are: the female ovum, the male sperm, and the karma-energy (*kammavega*), which, in the Suttas is metaphorically called '*gandhabba*', i.e. 'ghost'. This karma-energy is sent forth by the dying individual at the moment of his death. Father and mother only provide the necessary physical material for the formation of the embryonic body. With regard to the characteristic features, the tendencies and faculties lying latent in the embryo, the Buddha's teaching may be explained in the following way: The dying individual with his whole being convulsively clinging to life, at the very moment of his death, sends forth karmic energy which, like a flash of lightning, hits at a new mother's womb ready for conception. Thus, through the impinging of the karmic-energies on ovum and sperm, there arises, just as a precipitate, the so-called primary cell. . . . Hence we may say that the present life-process (*uppattibhava*) is the objectification of the corresponding pre-natal karma-process (*kammabhava*), and the future life-process is the objectification of the corresponding present karma-process. Thus, nothing transmigrates from the one life to the next.[4]

At death the consciousness perishes, only to give birth to another consciousness in a subsequent birth. This renewed life-flux inherits all past experiences. This new being is neither absolutely the same as the past one because of its different composition, nor totally different, being the identical strain of karmic-energy. (*Na ca so na ca añño* – 'he is neither the same nor another.')

Buddhist lore abounds in similes which help to clarify this paradox that the one who is born is neither the previous one nor yet another. The following are a few of these similes, some of which are modern.

(*a*) Like a seal pressed upon wax at the moment of death the karma-energy of a person is passed over to the soft wax of a new existence in another womb.

(*b*) When a man lights a light from another, one light does not pass over to the other.

(*c*) A sound produces air-vibrations which, by impinging on the acoustic organ of another man, produce a sound, which is purely a subjective sensation. No transmigration of a sound-sensation takes place (e.g. echo).

(*d*) A wave hastens over the ocean surface, rising and falling each time by the transmission of energy. One wave does not pass into the other, but the impact of the one gives rise to the other.

(*e*) When a boy learns a verse of poetry from a teacher, the verse does not pass from the teacher to the boy.

(*f*) Light in an electric bulb is only the outward visible manifestation of invisible electric energy. The bulb may break and the light may be extinguished, but the current remains and the light may be reproduced in another bulb.

(*g*) *Karma* is like a cable running unseen under the surface of the sea and emerging every now and again above the surface manifesting itself to our physical sight. Each emergence is what we call a 'lifetime', which in reality is the stretch of the cable's whole length, and the end is the completion of 'the cable of *kamma*', and not the mere termination of one of the manifestations of a portion of the *kamma-cable*.

(*h*) The birth-process of a butterfly is another illustration. It was first an egg and then it became a caterpillar. Later it developed into a chrysalis, and finally evolved into a butterfly. The butterfly is neither the same as, nor totally different from, the caterpillar. Here there is continuity of the flux of life.

The transition of the flux is instantaneous. There is no room for an intermediate state. Rebirth takes place immediately, and there is no difference in time, whether one is born in a heaven as a *deva* or in a state of misery as an animal or as a human being.

4. THE LAST MENTAL ACT

A *kamma*, either meritorious or demeritorious, is presented to every dying man, indicating the place in which he will be reborn. This *kamma* may arise in his mind in symbolic form, such as hell-fire, daggers and knives, forests, mountainous regions, a mother's womb, beautiful scenes or celestial mansions. However, if the indications of the place in which one is destined to be reborn are bad, they can be changed into good. This can be done by influencing the thoughts of the dying man. His good thoughts can act as a proximate *kamma* and counteract the influence of the reproductive *kamma*, which would otherwise determine his subsequent birth. It is the custom among Buddhists to remind a dying person of the good deeds which he has done during his life and to show him objects, such as the robes of a monk, to indicate that these will be offered to the monks on his behalf, so that, by the merit thus gained, he may be born in a happy world.

Taking for the object of the dying-thought one of the above, a thought process runs its course even if the death is instantaneous. It is said that even a fly crushed by a hammer on the anvil also experiences in that short second such a process of thought before it actually dies. This last thought is the mental act of transitive causation.

The Buddhist belief is that as a rule the thought, volition, or desire which is extremely strong during lifetime, becomes predominant at the point of death and conditions the subsequent birth. In this last thought is present a special potentiality. When the potential energy of this Reproductive Kamma is exhausted the organic activities of the material form, in which is corporealised the life-force, ceases even before the approach of old age. About this last conscious act Buddhaghosa writes:

> He who has no clear idea of death, or of rebirth, and does not master the fact that death is the dissolution of the five factors (mind and body) and that rebirth is the appearance of the five factors, concludes that a living entity deceases and transmigrates into another 'body' . . . No elements of being transmigrate from the last existence into the present, nor do they appear in the present existence without causes in the past existence. For at the hour of death, the last conscious act is as a man who, to cross a ditch, swings himself over by a rope hung on a tree above him. Yet he does not really alight, for, while the last conscious act dies away (and this is called 'passing'), another conscious act arises in a new life, and this is called 'rebirth' or conception. But it is to be understood that the latter conscious act did not come into the present life from the previous life. We must also understand that it is only to causes contained in the old existence that its present appearance is due.[5]

5. THE BHAVAṄGA THEORY

Behind the idea of the last conscious act is the *bhavanga* theory, which first appears in the *Milinda Pañha* without an antecedent history in the Pali Canon. It was a concept borrowed from the Sarvāstivāda Abhidharma (where it originally meant a link in the causal chain), in order to answer the question relating to personality and survival. This was the question that King Milinda asked the Monk Nāgasena. In answering, Nāgasena used the term *bhavaṅga*. E. R. Sarathchandra, commenting on how this word came to be adopted into Buddhism, says:

> Whether the Abhidhamma scholiasts were aware that they were reintroducing *vijñana* into Buddhism and using it in an unauthorised sense or not, they gave the word *bhavaṅga* the same meaning of 'factor of existence', *bhava* plus *aṅga*. In fact, the tradition of *bhavaṅga* as the cause of existence seems to have exerted so much influence that both commentators of the Abhidhammatthasangaha, Sumangala and Sāriputta Sangha-rājah, force into the word *aṅga* the meaning of cause and explain *bhavaṅga* as the cause of unbroken continuity of the individual in various existences. . . . Hence Buddhaghosa and his successors connect up *bhavaṅga* of an individual at death with his *bhavaṅga* at rebirth, and thus establish his continuity throughout his wanderings in saṃsāra.[6]

The *Bhavaṅga* theory found its way into the Abhidhamma and was picked up by Buddhaghosa (5th century A.D.), who used it as a synonym for *viññāna*) and equated it with rebirth consciousness (*paṭisandhi viññāṇa*). Buddhaghosa explains this as follows:

> As soon as rebirth-consciousness (in the embryo at the time of conception) has ceased, there arises a similar subconsciousness with exactly the same object, following immediately upon rebirth-consciousness and being the result of this or that karma (volitional action done in a former birth and remembered there at the moment before death). And again a further similar state of subconsciousness arises. Now, as long as no other consciousness arises to interrupt the continuity of the life-stream, so long the life-stream, like the flow of a river, rises in the same way again and again, even during dreamless sleep and at other times. In this way one has to understand the continuous arising of those states of consciousness in the life-stream.[7]

Anuruddha, who lived probably in the eleventh or twelfth century, sought to undergird the psychology of transmigration with the concept of the 'Stream of Being'. In *Abhidhammatthasangaha* (Compendium of Philosophy) he says:

> The Stream of Being, then, is an indispensable condition or factor; the *sine qua non* of present conscious existence; it is the *raison d'être* of individual life; it is the life-continuum; it is, as it were, the background on which thought-pictures are drawn. It is comparable to the current of a river when it flows calmly on, unhindered by any obstacle, unruffled by any wind, unrippled by any wave; and neither receiving tributary waters, nor parting with its content to the world. And when that current is opposed by any obstacle of thought from the world within, or perturbed by any tributory stream of the senses from the world without, then processes of cognition (*vīthicittas*) arise. But it must not be supposed that the stream of being is a sub-plane from which thoughts rise to the surface. There is juxtaposition of momentary states of consciousness, subliminal and supraliminal, throughout a life-time and from existence to existence. But there is no superposition of such states.
>
> Life, then, in the Buddhist view of things, is like an ever-changing river, having its source in birth, its goal in death, receiving from the tributary streams of sense constant accretions to its flood, and ever dispensing to the world around it the thought-stuff it has gathered by the way.[8]

Anuruddha speaks of a four-fold process of correlation in this continuum of mental states:

> Each mental state is related to the next in at least four different modes of relation (*paccaya*): – Proximity (*anantara*), Contiguity (*samanantara*), Absence (*n'atthi*), and Abeyance (*avigata*). This fourfold correlation is understood to mean that each expired state renders service (*upakāra*) to the next. In other words, each, on passing away, gives up the whole of its energy (*paccaya-satti*) to its successor. Each successor, therefore, has all the potentialities of its predecessors, and more.[9]

From this it is seen that in the thought of Anuruddha, the causal process consists in the individual transmission of potentiality. Thus the image of the 'stream' provides an identity of a sort; it is the idea of a thing on the ground of its continuity. Hence there is no conscious subject behind consciousness, no actor apart from action, no percipient apart from perception, no identity apart from continuity.

On the basis of this discussion let us now attempt to restate the Theravāda position in relation to two persistent questions: (1) If there is no self or soul who is it that is reborn? (2) How can you deny the self and yet assert moral responsibility, which *karma* implies?

To the first question the traditional Theravāda answer is that the person who is reborn is neither the one who died nor another (*na ca so na ca añño*). At death, consciousness perishes only to give rise to another consciousness in a subsequent re-becoming. The moment of dying begets the moment of consciousness in the womb and passes on its heritage of *karma*. The renewed life-flux inherits all past experiences. Each successor 'has all the potentialities of the predecessor and more'. The new being is neither absolutely the same as the past (because of its different composition), nor is it totally different (because it becomes within the identical strain of Karma-energy).

If there is no identifiable self or soul, can there be moral responsibility? The Theravāda answer often given to this second question is, that there *is* moral responsibility, because there is an identity and continuity of process. In the life-stream, the *karma*-energy strain belongs to no one else but the successor in the stream of being. Buddhism is thus seen to be a process philosophy and has affinities with the process philosophy of A. N. Whitehead and Charles Hartshorne. But there are significant differences too, which will be seen in the discussion that follows.

6. SELF-IDENTITY AND PROCESS PHILOSOPHY

A. N. Whitehead, the father of modern process philosophy, and Charles Hartshorne, his pupil and the foremost interpreter of his master's thought,[10] hold that all life is a process of becoming in which there can be no absolute and separable self-identity in the form of a persisting 'entity'. As Hartshorne has put it:

The only strict concrete identity is seen as belonging to the momentary self, the true unit of personal existence, as Hume and James rediscovered long after the Indians, Chinese, and Japanese. (Alas, the rediscovery included considerable repetition of the radical pluralism which plagued the Buddhists.) Each momentary self is a new actuality, however intimately related to its predecessors. It is self-enjoyed rather than self-interested. All aim beyond the present is interest taken by one momentary self in others. A kind of 'altruism' is thus the universal principle, self-interest being but the special case in which the other momentary selves in question form with the present self a certain chain or sequence. But this chain has not absolute claim upon its own members. Only the cosmic Life has absolute claims.[11].

In the light of this philosophical framework, Hartshorne finds the Buddhist view of the self more acceptable than some others:

> One may view the self or soul in three ways. There is the conventional notion that each of us is, or has, an identical soul from birth to death, or even prior to birth and after death. There is the doctrine of Hindu monism, that plurality of selves is in some sense only appearance, since the primary reality is beyond numerical diversity: hence the saying, *That art thou* – each of us is Brahma.
>
> There is finally the Buddhistic view, or the somewhat similar, but much later doctrine of David Hume and William James, recently revised by Whitehead, according to which each of us is a numerically new actuality every moment. Although I recognize some validity in each of these theories, it is the Buddhist-Whiteheadian doctrine which seems to me most capable of expressing the truth in them all.[12]

Whitehead and Hartshorne are agreed in denying any absolute self-identity throughout any series constituting a living being. A person consists of a series of momentary selves, each intimately related to the preceding self. 'The only strict concrete identity', as Hartshorne has put it, 'is seen in belonging to the momentary self'; and the 'being' of the self consists in its becoming. This is the principle of process philosophy.

This language is very Buddhistic and quite likely Whitehead and Hartshorne are consciously or unconsciously influenced by Buddhist thought, and up to a point there is much agreement between Buddhist and Whiteheadian process philosophy. But Hartshorne sees an inadequacy and an ambiguity in Buddhism. He applauds Buddhism for the advantage it has in being free from the individualism that characterises traditional Christian thought –

> But this advantage has been paid for by a certain negativism, a certain inadequacy, or at least ambiguity, in the Buddhist view of the values of existence. This defect does not derive from the fact that Buddhism is a philosophy of becoming and events, rather than of being and substances. It is connected instead with a certain radical pluralism in the Buddhist conception of event. Some Buddhists tried to defend a doctrine of the present reality of the past, but they failed to carry full conviction, and the reason may have been that they spoke in the same breath of the reality of past and also of future events.[13]

To appreciate this criticism we should understand what the word 'event' means, as used by Hartshorne and Whitehead. It is a word borrowed from quantum mechanics according to which the world consists not of things but of *events*, each having a momentary duration of a single pulse of a 'quantum' of energy radiated by an electron.[14] Unlike the Buddist theory of moments, these *events* are interdependent and inter-penetrating. Thus a person consists not of disconnected moments but of interdependent yet momentary *events* in a series, each intimately related to its predecessors and successors. The universe and everything in it is interdependent, everything depending on everything else and affecting each other and absorbing influences from the total environment, including God. The absorbing of influences is called 'prehension', which literally means grasping or seizing and need not be a conscious act as in 'apprehension', a word which Whitehead avoided. According to him even inanimate things can 'prehend'. He describes 'prehension' as follows:

> Every prehension consists of three factors: (a) the 'subject'which is prehending, namely, the actual entity in which that prehension is a concrete element; (b) the 'datum' (or object), which is prehended; (c) the 'subjective form' which is *how* that subject prehends that datum.[15]

It is by 'prehension' that permanence and personal identity is preserved. Whitehead identifies this permanence with the emergence of *value* in a world of perpetual change. Here we find a

fundamental difference between Buddhist and Whiteheadian process thought. Whitehead felt the need for preserving personal
identity; and in so doing, as Hartshorne points out, he even spoke of
personal immortality:

> It remains true that to Whitehead immortality is 'personal' in a
> literal sense. For all that is known to be actual of any human
> personality is the life of that person while on earth. And all this
> actuality, as actuality of experience – and what is value beyond
> all experience? – is just what, according to Whitehead, is immor-
> talized in the all-receptive unity of God.
>
>   Nothing is more personal about a man than his concrete
> experiences – which 'perish, and yet live for evermore' – in the
> divine, supremely personal life.[16]

Thus to make sense of process philosophy the idea of God had to be
brought in, in order to safeguard 'personal value'. As Hartshorne
puts it:

> We can, in the profoundest sense, 'live forever' if, and only if, we
> are cherished by an imperishable and wholly clear and distinct
> retrospective awareness which we may call the memory of God.[17]

Thus we see that without an ontology in which 'personal value' is
preserved 'forever', a process philosophy cannot have much
meaning. As Paul Tillich says:

> A process philosophy which sacrifices the persisting identity of
> that which is in process, sacrifices the process itself, its continuity,
> the relation of what is conditioned to the conditions, the inner
> aim (*telos*) which makes a process a whole. Bergson was right
> when he combined the *élan vital*, the universal tendency toward
> self-transcendence, with duration, with continuity and self-
> conservation in the temporal flux.[18]

In the Buddhist theory of becoming, personal value in the sense of
self-conservation, does not appear to be preserved, and this is what
seems to have led to the search for a principle of self-identity.

6 The Quest for Self-identity

I. PERSONALIST THEORIES

From very early times until the present day, the Theravāda interpretation of *anattā* has been the subject of much controversy. The common man finds it unintelligible and incompatible with his strong belief in rebirth. Thus throughout the history of Buddhism there has been a quest for a concept of the identity and continuity of the self that steers clear of nihilism and eternalism. This gave rise to different schools of thought that sought to circumvent the difficulties inherent in the doctrine of *anattā*. As Edward Conze remarks:

> Among all the tenets of Buddhism none has occasioned more controversy and misunderstanding than the *anātman* theory, which suggests that nowhere can a 'self' be apprehended. The prospect of complete self-extinction, welcomed by the true Buddhist, seems so bleak and arid to many students of the Dharma that they dream up a 'true Self' which, they say, will be realized by the extinction of the false, empirical self. This misinterpretation has proved so popular in Europe that one may be tempted to regard it as either an expression of the typical concern of modern Europeans for 'individuality' and 'personality', or as a remnant of the Christian belief in an immortal 'soul'. In fact it is not confined to European Christians or ex-Christians. Everywhere, even in India, it voices the murmuring of the unregenerate Adam when faced with the more magnificent vistas of Buddhist thought. Two centuries after the Buddha's Nirvāna it gave rise to the sect of the Puggalavādins.[1]

(a) The burden and the burden-bearer

The Puggalavādins or Personalists argued, in the first place, that it was absurd to deny the reality of the person and yet assert the theory of *karma* and rebirth. 'If the self is not real', they asked, 'who then remembers, who recognizes things, who recites and memorises

49

books, who repeats the texts . . . ?' There must be an 'I', they asserted, ' which first experiences, and then remembers what it has done. If there were none, how could one possibly remember what one has done?' The Buddha, they said, was able to recall his former lives, because there was a continuity of the same self, so that he was able to say, 'This sage Sunetra who existed in the past, that Sunetra was I.'

The Personalists raised the question of moral responsibility and argued that there could be no justice in the world, if the one who acts is not the same as the one who reaps his reward or punishment according to his *karma*. There must be, they insisted, an identifiable agent of actions; there must be a knower, if there is knowledge. If knowledge were impersonal and momentary, the Buddha could not be omniscient, they argued. They used the *Burden Sutra* to give weight to their argument.

> I will teach you, O priests, the bearer of the burden, the taking up of the burden, and the laying down of the burden. And what, O priests, is the burden? Reply should be made that it is the five attachment groups (*khandhas*). And what are the five? They are the five aggregates.[2]

An interpreted version of the *Burden Sutra*, 'which has been a favourite also with those who have attempted to revive the Personalist position in recent years', as Conze says, is found in Yasomitra's Vyākhyā to the *Abhidharmakosa*.

> I will teach you the burden, its taking up, its laying down, and the bearer of the burden (*bhāra-hāram*). The five *khandhas* (which are the range) of grasping are the burden. Craving takes up the burden. The renunciation of craving lays it down. The bearer of the burden is the person. This venerable man, with such and such a name, born so and so, of such and such a clan, who sustains himself on this or that food, experiences these pleasures and pains, lives for just so long, stays here for just so long, terminates his life-span in just this way.[3]

Apparently, this reference in the *Burden Sūtra* was the basis for the Personalists to claim that the person or self was clearly identifiable and distinct from the five *khandhas*. If there was no distinction, and the *khandhas* and the burden were identical, one would have to come to the logical conclusion that the burden carries itself; the burden itself is the bearer of the burden. This is of course absurd. However, they had to reconcile their theory of the self with the doctrine of *anattā*, for they claimed that they in no way rejected this doctrine preached by the Buddha. To explain how they could maintain this claim they evolved the theory of 'correlation'.

(b) The theory of correlation
According to the theory of correlation, the *Puggala* is 'neither identical with the *skandhas*, nor is he in the *skandhas*, nor outside them,' but 'the person can be conceived in with the *skandhas* which have been appropriated at any given time inwardly.' Taking the analogy of fire, they said that, just as fire and fuel exist together in correlation and never apart from each other, so the self exists in correlation with the *skandhas*; and just as fire has a nature of its own, namely heat, and an activity of its own, namely burning, so the self has a nature and activity of its own. Just as fire manifests itself through and co-exists with the fuel, so the self manifests itself through and co-exists with the *skandhas*, not as a separate entity, but as a kind of 'structural unity'.[4] In contrast to the orthodox view, the Personalists held that the self was practically real. The orthodox teachers maintained that the term *attā* is used in the conventional sense and not in the ontological sense of an ultimate reality (*paramattha*) and that this self could not be perceived or 'got at' (*upalabhyate*). In contrast, the Personalists maintained that the self or puggala 'can be got at' (*upalabhata*) as a reality in the ultimate sense (*paramatthena*), and that it can be an object of true experience (*sacchikata*).[5]

(c) Pseudo-selves
The urge to deviate from the strict orthodox interpretation of *anattā* and the search for some principle of identity and continuity of the self was strongly felt in many other sections of the early Buddhist communities. Conze says,

> So strong indeed is the practical and theoretical need for the assumption of a permanent factor in connection with the activities of a 'person', that in addition to the *Puggalavādins* other schools also felt obliged to introduce it more or less furtively in a disguised form, though the 'self' remained taboo all the time. These 'pseudo-selves' are not easy to study, partly because there is

little precise information, and partly because the concepts themselves are distinctly indefinite.[6]

This urge was so strong that the *Sautrāntika* sect went to the extent of teaching that the *skandhas* transmigrated from one life to another. Thus the empirical self was given the status of the real self. This gave rise to theories about the *skandhas*. The *Mahīsāsakas* distinguished three kinds of *skandhas*; those which are momentary, those which endure during one life, and those which last until the end of *Saṃsāra*. It may be because this theory sounded somewhat materialistic that the *Sautrāntikas* postulated an incorruptible 'seed' of 'goodness', an innate, indestructible and perfectly pure factor which persists through all the change until emancipation is found in *Nirvāna*. Support for this view was found in a sentence quoted in the *Abhidharmakosa*. 'I see this extremely subtle seed of salvation like a seam of gold hidden in a metal-bearing rock.' The *Yogācārins*, in agreement with the *Sautrāntikas*, maintained that there are some innate wholesome and indestructible *dharmas* which persist intact in the form of 'seeds' in the 'continuity', these 'seeds' giving rise to new and wholesome *dharmas* under favourable conditions.

It is clear from this brief survey that throughout the history of Buddhist thought there has been an instinctive belief in an identifiable and permanent 'self' which the different schools tried to smuggle in but which the Theravādins persistently resisted. Th. Stcherbatsky points out how, in the history of Buddhist thought, attempts were made to reintroduce the idea of the 'soul' through some back-door:

> Just as in the Hinayāna period the categories of substance and quality, although officially banned, always tended to re-appear through some back-door, just so in the idealistic period the notion of a soul, although continued to be officially repudiated – Buddhists still remain the champions of soullessness – nevertheless haunted the domain of Buddhist philosophy and tended to introduce itself in some form or other into the very heart of Buddhism.[7]

The outlawing of the notion of the soul has in recent times led either to the rejection of the belief in rebirth as incompatible with the doctrine of *anattā* or to the attempt to smuggle in the idea of the soul in one form or other. We shall briefly consider some of the recent developments.

2. THE SELF AS COLLECTIVE KARMA

1. J. G. Jennings, in his book *The Vedantic Buddhism of the Buddha* (in which he says he seeks to rediscover the original teachings of the Buddha), interprets *karma* in a collective sense and 'rebirth', or rather rebecoming (*Punabbhava*), in the sense of the transmission of *karma* to succeeding generations and not to individuals. He suggests that the traditional idea of rebirth, which is completely incompatible with the doctrine of *anattā*, was later accommodated by Buddhists under pressure from Hinduism. Accordingly he rejects all passages in the Pitakas referring to rebirth as later additions, and from what remains he contends that Buddhism is exclusively a system of ethical conduct motivated by a sense of collective responsibility, which the doctrine of *anattā* serves to emphasise by exposing the absurdity of selfish conduct, for, since there is no self, self-centred conduct is futile.

Jennings' arguments for rejecting the doctrine of rebirth are as follows:

(*a*) There is no phrase or word that can be claimed as supporting the doctrine of rebirth in the First Sermon, the *Dhammacakkappavattana* Sutta, which contains the core of the Buddha's teaching. The word *ponobhavikā*, found in this Sermon, usually translated as 'causing a re-existence or rebirth', is, Jennings asserts, 'so startlingly irrelevant in the sermon that it would appear to have been added by a later hand.[8] But if this word is translated as 'tending to arise again, repeating itself, recurring (that is, causing the rebirth of itself, not of the individual)', thus using it as an epithet for *taṇhā*, then 'it is fully in accord with the doctrine of altruistic responsibility.'[9]

(*b*) In three of the most important *suttas* – namely, the famous *Tevijja Sutta*, in which the way to union with Brahman is explained; the equally famous *Mahā-parinibbāna Sutta*, in which the faith is summarised and which was repeated in every town and village during the Buddha's last tour; and the well-known *Singālovāda Sutta* which lays down the duties of laymen – 'the subject of transmigration receives no mention whatsoever.'[10]

(*c*) Rebirth is not mentioned in the crucial passages which relate to the essentials of the *Dhamma*.[11]

(*d*) In the conversion sermons, which led to the conversion of about sixty people and in which probably the teaching of the Buddha is found in its purest form, there is nothing to establish that the Buddha accepted the doctrine of rebirth.[12] The word *sagga* or heaven found in these sermons and elsewhere means 'light', that is, the bliss of perfect enlightenment, and not a realm where people are reborn.

(*e*) In the instructions to the First Missionaries, which is a very remarkable document, there is not even a hint regarding *Saṃsāra* (rebirth) and personal *karma*.[13]

(*f*) The view that sorrow and joy are caused by what has been done before (*pubbe kata-hetu*) is definitely called heresy (*titthāyatana*). Thus *karma* in a previous birth is ruled out.[14]

(*g*) In the Edicts of the Emperor Asoka (circa 250 B.C.), who accepted the essentials of the teaching of the Buddha, there is no trace of the doctrine of Rebirth.[15]

All this leads Jennings to the conclusion that,

> . . . the theory of personal rewards and punishments in successive lives is radically inconsistent with his [the Buddha's] characteristic doctrine of No Self, or the impermanence of the individuality (*sabbe dhammā anattā*) and with altruism, being in essence individualistic.[16]

Jennings maintains that while the Buddha rejected the idea of rebirth, he accepted the then prevalent doctrine of *karma* in a different sense:

> Disbelieving in the permanence of the individual soul he could not accept the Hindu doctrine of *karma* implying the transmigration of the soul at death to a new body; but believing fully in moral responsibility and the consequence of all acts, words and thoughts, he fully accepted the doctrine of *karma* in another sense, implying the transmission of the effects of actions from one generation of men to all succeeding generations.[17]

Jennings points out that the idea that the individual disappears at death, but the aggregates of his actions or *karma* cause the birth of a new individual – as a flame is transmitted – until *karma* ceases, is a later attempt at reconciling the doctrine of *anattā* with the theory of reincarnation. He says,

> . . . it is not established that he (the Buddha) himself assumed that the aggregate of one individual's actions miraculously creates upon his death a new individual to bear the consequences.

Therefore he concludes:

> Allowing that the reconciliation is later, it may be assumed that the Buddha, teaching the doctrine of no-permanent-soul, moral responsibility, and altruism, taught a doctrine of altruistic responsibility or collective *Karma*, according to which every action, word and thought of the individual, transient though he be, brings forth inevitably consequences to be suffered or enjoyed by others in endless succeeding generations.[18]

In this connection, mention should be made of a recent book by T. A. P. Ariyaratne, who holds a similar view to that of Jennings. Asserting that all Buddha's views have a rational basis, he rejects the theory of rebirth as rationally incompatible with the doctrine of *anattā*. According to him, man has only one span of life to live, with death as the final stroke of extinction. This, he holds, far from being a reason to 'eat, drink and be merry, for tomorrow we die', is rather 'a reminder to all of the importance of striving earnestly to aim at forgetting the self.'[19] This, he says, is the essence of the doctrine of *anattā*.

3. THE SELF AS ĀTMAN

A. K. Coomaraswamy, in his book *Hinduism and Buddhism*, contends that the Buddhist and the Vedāntic teaching are in agreement; the Buddha and Sankara say the same things although in different ways:

> The Vedānta and Buddhism are in complete agreement that, while there is transmigration, there are no individual transmigrants. All that we can see is the operation of cause, and so much the worse for us if we see in this fatally determined nexus our 'Self'.[20]

The difference in expressing the same truth is that, while 'in Brahmanical terms "ignorance is of who we are", in Buddhist language it is of "what we are not".'[21] But this negative way of speaking does not mean "There is no self."[22] Nor is it anywhere asserted. The Buddha used the 'via negativa' in order to drive home to his disciples the Vedāntic truth that the real Self cannot be identified with the five aggregates which are transient. Thus,

> Our constitution and that of the world is repeatedly analysed, and as each of the five physical and mental factors of transient personality, with which the 'untaught manyfolk' identify 'themselves' is listed, the pronouncement follows, 'That is not myself.'[23]

The phrase 'That is not myself' (*na me so attā*), so frequently occuring especially in the *Anattalakkhaṇa Sutta*, the Second Sermon of the Buddha, is, Coomaraswamy asserts, a denial only of the false self but not of the Supreme Self of the Upanishads:

> It is of course true that Buddha denied the existence of a soul or self, in the narrow sense of the word, but this is not what our writers mean to say . . . What they mean to say is that Buddha denied the immortal and Supreme Self of the Upanishads. And that is palpably false. For he frequently speaks of this self or spirit, and nowhere more explicitly than in the repeated formula 'na me so atta' (that is not myself), excluding body and components of empirical consciousness, a statement to which the words of Sankara are peculiarly apposite, 'Whenever we deny something unreal, it is with reference to something real'.[24]

In support of this contention Coomaraswamy cites the incident recorded in the Mahāvagga[25] of a party of young men who went on a picnic with their wives, one of them taking with him a prostitute because he was unmarried. This prostitute, while others were amusing themselves, made off with some of their valuables. The young man pursued her and coming across the Buddha asked him if he had seen her, to which the Buddha replied, 'What now, young man, do you think? Which were the better, for you to go tracking the woman, or to go tracking the Self? (*ātmānam gavis*).' The only possible meaning of the word self in this context, Coomaraswamy argues, is that given to it in the Vedānta teaching – the *Atman*, the Supreme Self.[26]

Coomaraswamy's view is not new. Many other scholars have advocated this view.[27] But coming from a man of such high erudition and standing in the world of Buddhist scholarship it commands attention. Many feel that this is the only solution to the problem with which Buddhism is faced, but Orthodox Theravādins have constantly resisted this tendency to hinduise, so to speak, the Buddha's teachings. Some of them maintain that Buddhism was not a reform movement within Hinduism as has often been claimed, and, far from being a specific expression of the Brahmanistic thinking, was a radical protest against Brahmanism with contradistinctive teachings.

4. THE SELF AS IMMANENT DEITY IN MAN

In opposition to the view expressed by Coomaraswamy, C. A. F. Rhys Davids maintained that the Buddha adopted a positive attitude to life in contrast to the world-and-life-negating attitude of the Vedānta. For her the word *atta* meant the immanent deity in man which made him a real self. Her view is at variance with her husband's, who more or less was in agreement with the Theravāda interpretation of the doctrine of *anattā*.[28] She says that the notion of *anattā*, 'the frightful canker of the Not-man,' arose only in the monkish tradition, while the Buddha's message was for Everyman – a folk-gospel.

> In a 'folk-gospel' like that message, we should expect to find in its quest something which was (1) the man seeking to attain, and finally attaining, his welfare as man, not a welfare without man; man must be in it; (2) a quest which is positive, not negative; (3) a quest which is not something as yet inconceivable by man, but is something which he can even now comprehend, or at least conceive.[29]

The *anattā* doctrine and the concept of *Nirvāna*, according to Mrs Rhys Davids, fail this three-fold test. If the human quest is to be real, man, the self, must really be in it. So she insists that the original goal of Buddhism was *Attha* (Sanskrit *Artha*), a positive goal, rather than *Nirvāna*. Such a goal can be sought after only if the path is and also the man who walks on it, and the goal is and the person who enters it.

Mrs Rhys Davids asserts that this positive outlook underlies the 'folk-evangel' of the Buddha:

> Man in religion is a seeker, essentially and before all else a seeker; that man, in this seeking, may word his quest not necessarily in a word which tries to convey something he cannot yet conceive, but as a Better which, for the time being, is for him a Best. And now we see how in *attha* we get those three features suitable for a folk-evangel, which we did not get in Nirvana. *Attha* is essentially a standpoint of the man, not of one who in gaining it ceases somehow to be man. It is the man who is valuing: this is my aim. It becomes meaningless if, in winning it he wanes out. . . . Second, the word is positive, not a negative. It is that which is sought for, is to be won. It is not something that is a NOT. Lastly, it is not something which having won, a man judges to be so 'void' that he cannot value. It is ever true as being that which man, in seeking, ever figures as the Best, the Most he can as yet conceive.[30]

How then did this positive affirmation of the self and the goal drop out and give place to the doctrine of *anattā* and the negative concept of *Nirvāna*? Mrs Rhys Davids' theory is that this happened under the negativist trend in Monastic Buddhism. She explains the process as follows:

> The dropping out of *attha* is preceded by that tragic worsening in values, the dropping out of 'the man', that is, 'the self'. We know that, in drifting apart from the mother-teacher, Brahmanism – the immanence of God as in and of the man — early Buddhism first cut out deity from the term *attā*, then cut out the reality of the *attā* himself, a decadent process covering centuries.
>
> With *atta* and the *attha* dropped from its quest of the ideal, Buddhism built over these buried stones the rococo superstructure which the founders of the movement would have pain and difficulty in recognizing and of which they would certainly not have approved. The *attha* which they taught was not *nibbāna*, a vanishing Less in a vanishing *attā*. It was a persisting living on in that more which saw the quest as a man becoming more in the worlds. . . .[31]

Mrs Rhys Davids has been severely criticised by Buddhist scholars for her unorthodox views. She is alleged to have had spiritualistic leanings which are supposed to have influenced her thinking, and she is accused of trying to read into Buddhism the philosophy of the twentieth century represented by Bergson and Coué. Her conclusions are considered to be conjectures or hypotheses in keeping with her peculiar leanings. Nevertheless she holds a very significant place in Buddhist scholarship as a penetrating questioner, who asks the right questions. Her writings have had such a great influence that, it is remarked, we no longer 'read the Buddhist scriptures like Fundamentalists'.

5. SELF AS A CHANGELESS PRINCIPLE – SPIRIT

Christmas Humphreys is one of the foremost influential exponents of Buddhism in the West. While he is in agreement with the doctrine of *anattā* which 'states categorically that there is in man no permanent 'Immortal Soul' which eternally distinguishes one unit of life from another,'[32] he rejects the Theravāda interpretation of *anattā* as meaning an unqualified no-self.

> Unfortunately, the Buddhists of the Southern School have taken the word *anattā* to mean that there is no self other than the five *skandhas* described by the Buddha. There is no scriptural justification for such a view. Granted that none of the *skandhas*, nor their totality, is the Self, still less the SELF, for to identify oneself with the personality is to confuse the driver with the chariot, yet nowhere does the Blessed One deny that this personality is the instrument of a Self which, ever growing towards perfection, will only cease to need these instruments at the threshold of Nirvāna.[33]

In the above passage and elsewhere in his writings, Humphreys constantly speaks of a self as a changeless principle. 'Let us speak then' he says, 'of a form called SELF, the firstborn of the Nameless'. He explains what he means by this in terms of a changeless PRINCIPLE:

> Beyond all forms, all pairs of opposites, there dwells 'an Omnipresent, Eternal, Boundless and Immutable PRINCIPLE

on which all speculation is impossible, since it transcends the power of human conception, and could only be dwarfed by any human expression or similitude' (*Secret Doctrine*, H. P. Blavatsky, 1.14). The first radiation of this nameless PRINCIPLE, the first and lightest veil about the formless Life, and therefore the first and ultimate Form, is SELF. It has no nature, for it is beyond all predicates, and being the essence of Life it is the exclusive property of none. Its alone-begotten children are the Pairs of Opposites, the eldest, Life and Form, producing the Self and Not-Self respectively. But no man can conceive duality without conceiving three, for all things, being products of the mind, must have relationship, and this relationship reflects the SELF, the Higher Third which gave birth to the opposites.[34]

Humphreys goes on to speak of Body, Soul and Spirit in Pauline terms which he refers to as 'The Trinity of threefold Spirit'.

With this division of man into three, there appears the familiar 'Body, Soul and Spirit' of St. Paul, taking Body to include those factors which compose the 'personality', Soul to mean the nobler qualities of man which form his essential character, and Spirit as the Life which fills all forms alike and is the monopoly of none, we have a working analysis of man's constituents which may be reasonably called the self, the Self and the SELF respectively.[35]

This understanding of Spirit, Soul and Body is indeed most interesting, for it brings us very close to the biblical understanding of these three terms. Humphreys elaborates these further as follows.

About Spirit he says that this Ātman,

. . . so far from being that which distinguishes man from man, is actually the 'common denominator of all forms of life, and is hence the philosophic basis of the brotherhood of man. The degradation of this noble idea is paralleled in Christianity, in which the self-same teaching of St. Paul has been caricatured in the conception of an 'eternal soul' which distinguishes each man from his neighbour, and which will be either 'saved' or 'damned' at death according as the preponderance of his deeds in one short life has been good or bad. . . . This alone is eternal, but it is not an immortal entity, for 'there is no abiding principle in man'.[36]

He uses the term soul

> in the sense of a growing, evolving bundle of attributes or characteristics, forming 'character'. This it is which passes, by a process of causal impulse, from life to life on the long road to perfection.[37]

The term Body is

> used in the sense of 'personality', composed of the lower attributes or *skandhas*. The point to be made clear is that there is nothing in man which entitles him to say, 'I am this and you are that', through all eternity.
>
> It is this 'Heresy of Separateness' which causes the rival hatreds of the West, for, once established that 'I' am utterly different, separate from 'You', fratricidal wars in trade, politics, and in the open field will follow as a matter of course. Above the clamour of competitive strife the self-same Teaching of the Christ remains unheard.[38]

Attention should be drawn to Humphreys' idea of spirit as a relationship and thus 'the philosophic basis of the brotherhood of man'. This is a thoroughly biblical idea which is a heritage he has brought into his new-found faith and system of thinking. This relationship, Humphreys says, is not only within the brotherhood of man but also with an Absolute Reality understood in Buddhist terms. This is stated in the 'Twelve Principles of Buddhism' of the London Buddhist Society, of which Mr Humphreys is the President. He explains this as follows:

> Buddhism does not deny the existence of God or soul, though it places its own meaning on those terms. By God the Buddhist means THAT from which the universe was born, the Unborn of the Udāna, and by soul that factor in the thing called man which moves towards Enlightenment.[39]

He acknowledges that this is not in accord with the Theravāda teaching, which, according to him, was developed at a later point in history by the Sangha:

> . . . members of the Sangha at some point in history took it up-

on themselves to teach what the Buddha never taught, that there is no quality beyond the *skandhas* which is a reflection or manifestation, call it what you will, of THAT 'the Unborn', of which the universe as a whole is a partial and perishable expression.[40]

It is worthy of note that Humphreys emphasises the point that *anattā* is not a doctrine but a matter of experience:

> It has been wisely said that the nature of the Self is an experience and not a doctrine; that it must in other words be found as we tread the Way. Hence the Buddha's silence on the subject for it cannot be usefully described.[41]

Humphreys' view is not at all acceptable to Theravādins, nor is his view in harmony with the biblical view, although one gets the impression that it is, because he uses biblical terms. However, his emphasis on the social and existential dimensions of the self is of great significance and echoes biblical teaching.

7 Self-identity and Nibbāna

I. THE MEANING OF NIBBĀNA

(a) Extinction of desire

We come now to an inevitable question which is very frequently asked: What happens to the self finally? Will the self become extinct or lose its identity by being absorbed in the Absolute, or will self-identity be ultimately preserved? If in reality there is no immortal soul or self, what then is it that 'attains' *Nibbāna*?

The Pali term *Nibbāna* (Sanskrit *Nirvāna*) is composed of the particles '*Ni*' and '*Vāna*'. *Ni* is a particle implying negation and *Vāna* means weaving or craving. It is this craving that weaves a cord connecting one life with another. This is the meaning that the great commentator Anuruddha gives to the term: 'It is called *Nibbāna*, in that it is a "departure" from the craving which is called *vāna*, lusting.'[1] As long as the craving lasts one accumulates fresh karmic forces which bind one to the eternal cycle of birth and death. But when the cord is cut and all forms of craving are extirpated, the karmic forces cease to operate, thus ending the cycle of birth and death, and one attains *Nibbāna*.

Nibbāna is also explained as the extinction of the fire of lust (*rāga*), hatred (*dosa*) and delusion (*moha*). The fire simile is one of the favourite similes constantly employed by the Buddha and used by Buddhists to elucidate the meaning of *Nibbāna*. In the famous Fire-sermon the Buddha said:

> The whole world is in flames. By what fire is it kindled? By the fire of lust [*rāga*], of hatred [*dosa*] and of delusion [*moha*]. By the fire of birth, old age, death, pain, lamentation, sorrow, grief and despair it is kindled.[2]

The extinction of this fire is called *Nibbāna*. 'To him who has won freedom through the cessation of consciousness (*viññāna*) and the destruction of craving, the liberation of mind is (like) extinction (*parinibbāhi*) of a lamp.'³ 'By winning the highest purity you must be extinguished like a fire by water.'⁴ 'Kassapa meditates without fuel extinguished [*nibbuto*] among the burning, having attained the ultimate security, like a mass of fire extinguished' (*nibbuta*).⁵ When the Buddha passed away, Anuruddha his disciple uttered the memorable words:

> His mind was firm, without exhalation and inhalation. When the sage passed away, free from desire, having found peace, he endured pain with active mind: the liberation of mind was (like) the extinction of a lamp.⁶

The idea of extinction is also expressed in other passages without the use of the simile of fire:

> It is the complete cessation of that very 'thirst' (*taṇhā*), giving it up, renouncing it, emancipation from it, detachment from it.
>
> Calming of all conditioned things, giving up of all defilements, extinction of 'thirst', detachment, cessation, Nibbana.
>
> O bhikkhus, what is the Absolute (*Asaṃkhata*, Unconditioned)? It is, O bhikkhus, the extinction of desire (*rāgakkhayo*), the extinction of hatred (*dosakkhayo*), the extinction of illusion (*mohakkhayo*). This, O bhikkhus, is called the Absolute.
>
> O Rādha, the extinction of 'thirst' (*Taṇhakkhayo*) is Nibbāna.
>
> O bhikkhus, whatever there may be, things conditioned or unconditioned, among them detachment (*virāga*) is the highest. That is to say, freedom from conceit, destruction of thirst, the uprooting of attachment, the cutting off of continuity, the extinction of 'thirst' (*taṇhā*), detachment, cessation, Nibbāna.
>
> The abandoning and destruction of desire and craving for those Five Aggregates of Attachment: that is the cessation of *dukkha*.⁷

Even suicide is justified if there is no craving or desire for the Five Aggregates of Existence. This is well brought out in the story of Venerable Channa's suicide. Channa, who had attained Arahat-hood, fell ill with a fatal disease and was in great pain. Sāriputta, one of the greatest of the Buddha's disciples, accompanied by Mahā-Cunda, went to see Channa, to comfort him and give him whatever help he needed in his grave state of health. Channa declined any help, saying that he had everything he needed by way of food, medicine and attendance, and then declared: 'I am losing ground; my pains grow on me, I shall use the knife on myself; I have no wish to live.' This came as a shock to Sāriputta, who tried to dissuade him from such an act, which seemed to betray his great attainment. He asked Channa whether, after being a faithful disciple of the Buddha for so long and having attained Sainthood, he was still enslaved by the senses. Channa replied that he had no desire but the cessation of the Five Aggregates of Attachment.

Then Sāriputta admonished him, saying: 'You must think too, Channa, of the Lord's eternal teaching that agitation marks the enthralled; that the un-enthralled know no agitation; that, if there is serenity, that with serenity there is no craving; that without craving there is no round of rebirths; that without the round of rebirths there is not passing hence, no arising elsewhere; that without any passing hence, or arising elsewhere there is no further term in this world or elsewhere or both; and that thus alone is Ill (*Dukkha*) ended forever.'

So saying, Sāriputta and Mahā-Cunda left him, and, no sooner had they gone, than Channa used the knife on himself. Hearing about this, Sāriputta and Mahā-Cunda were greatly troubled and puzzled. So they went to the Buddha with the news and asked him what Channa's fate would be, because he desired to get rid of his body.

The Buddha replied that if a man 'divests' himself of his body because he desires another body, he is blameworthy. But, because Channa had no desire for another body he 'was blameless in using the knife upon himself'. The two inquirers were greatly pleased and 'rejoiced in what the Lord had said'.[8]

This form of extinction may seem intolerable to many, but to the Arahat the certainty that this is his last existence brings to him a sense of exquisite joy, and when he divests himself of his body he reaches *Parinirvāna* – the dreamless peace and happiness.

(b) Experience of happiness

Among the synonyms used for *Nibbāna*, some describe a state of peace and happiness that is experienced by those in whom the fire of desire has become extinct. Such are the synonyms *santaṃ* 'peace', *sivaṃ* 'happiness', *khemaṃ* 'security', *avyāpajjha* 'kindness' and the best-known *paramaṃsukhaṃ* 'highest bliss'. We also find hedonistic descriptions. It is said that the mortal who delights in *Nibbāna* (*nibbānābhiratho*), is freed from all *dukkha*.[9]

Nibbāna is an experience of self-negation resulting from the extinction of defilements leading to peace and happiness. We find a number of expressions of peace and happiness in the *Dhammapada*:

> Calm is his mind, calm is his speech, calm are his actions who, rightly knowing, is wholly freed from defilements perfectly peaceful, and equipoised.
>
> Whether in village or in forest, in vale or on hill, wherever Arahats dwell, delightful, indeed, is that spot.
>
> Delightful are the forests where worldlings delight not; the passionless will rejoice [therein], [for] they seek no sensual pleasures.
>
> Ah, happily do we live without hate amongst the hateful; amidst hateful men we dwell unhating.
>
> Ah, happily do we live in good health amongst the ailing; amidst ailing men we dwell in good health.
>
> Ah, happily do we live without yearning [for sensual pleasures] amongst those who yearn [for them]; amidst those who yearn [for them] we dwell without yearning.
>
> Ah, happily do we live, we who have no impediments. Feeders of joy shall we be even as the gods of the Radiant Realm.[10]

How can there be an experience of happiness if there is no 'experiencing' self? is a question that is often asked. This was the question that Udāyi asked Sāriputta when he once said: 'O friend, Nirvāna is happiness! Nirvāna is happiness!' Then Udāyi asked: 'But, friend Sāriputta, what happiness can it be if there is no sensation?' To this Sāriputta gave a paradoxical and classic answer: 'That there is no sensation itself is happiness.'

Here and now we can have this experience of happiness. Buddhism speaks of two stages or aspects of *Nibbāna*. (*a*) *Sa-upādi-sesa-nibbāna*, i.e. *Nibbāna* with the groups of existence, the five aggregates, still remaining after the extinction of all defilements (*Kilesa-parinibbāna*). (*b*) *An-upādi-sesa-nibbāna*, i.e. *Nibbāna* without the groups of existence remaining. This takes place with the death of the Arahat when the groups of existence also become extinct (*khandha-parinibbāna*).

What is it which maintains the Arahat in a bodily form until *parinirvāna* takes place? The usual answer is that the momentum of antecedent *kamma* carries on the physical existence even after the extinction of all the causes of existence, and this is expressed in a striking simile of the potter's wheel, which continues to turn for some time after the hand of the potter is removed.

(c) An ineffable paradox

The question as to whether the Arahat after death continues to live as a distinct individual was put to the Buddha: 'The person who has attained the goal, does he not exist or does he exist eternally without defect? Explain to me well, O Lord, as you understand it.' The answer the Buddha gave was neither negative nor affirmative. He simply said: 'The person who attained the goal is beyond measure' (*na pamāṇam atthi*).[11] On another occasion the Buddha gave a similar paradoxical answer which is recorded in the Brahmajāla Sutta:

> The outward form, brethren, of him who has won the truth (Tathāgata), stands before you, but that which binds him to rebirth [viz: *taṇhā*, thirst] is cut in twain. So long as his body shall last, so long do gods and men behold him. On the dissolution of the body, beyond the end of his life, neither gods nor men shall see him.[12]

The reason for such a paradoxical answer is that the terms 'exists' and 'ceases to exist' are misleading because they have a spacio-temporal connotation and are inapplicable to *Nirvāna*, which is beyond space and time and cannot be located (*na katthaci, na kuhiñci*). It therefore escapes conceptual formulation and literal description.

There was an interesting conversation between the Buddha and Vacchagotta concerning this very question. This wandering ascetic Vacchagotta approached the Buddha and questioned him as follows:

> But, Gotama, where is the Bhikkhu or Arahat who is delivered of mind reborn?
> Vaccha, to say that he is reborn would not fit the case.
> Then, Gotama, he is not reborn.
> Vaccha, to say that he is not reborn would not fit the case.
> Then, Gotama, he is both reborn and not reborn.
> Vaccha, to say that he is both reborn and not reborn would not fit the case.
> Then, Gotama, he is neither reborn nor not reborn.

Vaccha, to say that he is neither reborn nor not reborn would not fit the case.

Vaccha was baffled on hearing these seemingly inconsistent answers and in his bewilderment exclaimed: 'Gotama, I am at a loss to think on this matter, and I have become greatly confused.' To this the Buddha replied, and the conversation continued as follows:

Enough, O Vaccha. Be not at a loss to think on this matter and be not greatly confused. Profound, O Vaccha, is this doctrine, recondite and difficult of comprehension, good, excellent, and not to be reached by mere reasoning, subtle, and intelligible only to the wise, and it is a hard doctrine for you to learn who belong to another sect, to another faith, to another persuasion, to another discipline, and who sit at the feet of another teacher. Therefore, O Vaccha, I shall now question you, and do you make answer as may seem to you good. What think you, Vaccha? Suppose a fire were to burn in front of you, would you be aware that a fire was burning in front of you?

Gotama, if a fire were to burn in front of me, I should be aware that a fire was burning in front of me.

But suppose, Vaccha, someone were to ask you: 'On what does this fire that is burning in front of you depend?' What would you answer, Vaccha?

I would answer, O Gotama, it is on fuel of grass and wood that this fire burning in front of me depends.

But, Vaccha, if the fire in front of you were to become extinct, would you be aware that the fire in front of you had become extinct?

Gotama, if the fire in front of me were to become extinct, I would be aware that the fire in front of me had become extinct.

But, Vaccha, if someone were to ask you – 'In what direction has the fire gone, East or West, North or South?', what would you say, Vaccha?

The question would not fit the case, Gotama, for the fire depends on the fuel of grass and wood, and when the fuel has all gone, and it can get no other, being thus without nutriment it is said to be extinct.

In exactly the same way, Vaccha, all forms, sensations,

perceptions, mental activities and consciousness have been abandoned, uprooted, made like a palmyra stump, become extinct, and not liable to spring up in the future.

The Saint, O Vaccha, who has been released from what are styled the Five Aggregates, is deep, immeasurable like the mighty ocean. To say that he is reborn would not fit the case. To say that he is not reborn would not fit the case. To say that he is neither reborn nor not reborn would not fit the case.[13]

This ineffable paradox is epitomised in Buddhaghosa's memorable words:

> Here suffering exists, no sufferer is found;
> The deed is, but no doer of the deed is there;
> Nirvāna is, but not the man that enters it;
> The Path is, but no traveller on it is seen.[14]

2. INTERPRETATIONS OF THE MEANING OF NIBBĀNA

Perhaps there is no single subject in Buddhism on which more has been written than on *Nibbāna*. Over forty years ago de la Vallée Poussin remarked that already too much had been written about *Nirvāna*. Since then more has been written. But it is doubtful whether today we are clearer on the subject. Divergent views have been expressed in scholarly literature.

(a) Nibbāna as annihilation or extinction
Some reputed scholars like Oldenberg, Stcherbatsky, Burnouf and Paul Dahlke have come to the conclusion that, according to the Buddhist texts, *Nibbāna* is nothing but a negative state of complete annihilation, and Buddhism is therefore a philosophy of pessimism and despair. According to these scholars the doctrine of *anattā* 'precludes all possibility of survival', and the theory of selflessness is 'incompatible with any kind of survival' and therefore '*Nibbāna is annihilation*' (Poussin); it is 'absolute nothing' (Burnouf); it is 'simply extinction' (Rhys Davids). Dahlke frequently stresses this and in one place he writes: 'Only in Buddhism does the conception of freedom from pain remain purely a negative thing and not a positive in disguise – heavenly bliss.'[15]

Oldenberg, referring to the famous dialogue between the Buddha and Vacchagotta, quoted above, comes to the following conclusion:

> We see that the person who has framed this dialogue has in his thought very nearly approached the consequence, which leads to the negation of the ego. It may almost be said that, though probably he did not wish to express this consequence with overt consciousness, yet he has in fact expressed it. If the Buddha avoids the negation of the existence of the ego, he does so in order not to shock the weakminded hearer. Through shrinking from the question as to the existence or non-existence of the ego, is heard the answer, to which the premises of the Buddhist teaching tended: The ego is not; or, what is equivalent: Nirvāna is annihilation . . .[16]

(b) A positive ethical state

Over against this nihilistic view, Max Muller and Childers, after a careful examination of all the passages relating to *Nirvāna*, conclude that 'there is not one passage which would require that its meaning should be annihilation.'[17] As Max Muller says:

> Only in the hands of philosophers to whom Buddhism owes its metaphysics, does Nibbāna, through constant negations carried to an extreme degree by the exclusion and subtraction of all that is not Nibbāna, become at last an empty nothing, a philosophic myth.[18]

But the difficulty has always been to describe what this positive state is, and to reconcile it with the doctrine of *anattā*.

Rhys Davids and William Stede concluded that 'Nibbāna is purely and solely an ethical state, to be reached in this birth by ethical practices, contemplation and insight. It is therefore not transcendental.[19] . . . The ethical state called Nibbāna can only rise from within. It is therefore in the older texts compared to the fire going out, rather than to the fire being put out.'[20] *Nibbāna* is therefore 'nothing but "eternal salvation" after which the hearts of the religious yearn on the whole earth.'[21]

In support of this positive view Rhys Davids refers to some thirty-three designations of *Nibbāna*, such as everlasting (*ananta*); the Truth (*sacca*); the immeasurable (*appamāna*); supramundane (*lo-*

kuttara); stable (*dhuva*); uncompounded (*asaṃkhata*); the indiscernible (*anidassana*); the absolute (*kevala*).

Rhys Davids also collates from his wide knowledge of the Tripitaka a number of epithets which designate what *Nibbāna* is. Thus *Nibbāna* is described as: 'the harbour of refuge', 'the cool cave', 'the island amidst floods', 'the place of bliss', 'emancipation', 'liberation', 'safety', 'the supreme', 'the transcendental', 'the uncreated', 'the tranquil', 'the home of ease', 'the calm', 'the end of suffering', 'the medicine for all evil', 'the unshaken', 'the ambrosia', 'the immaterial', 'the imperishable', 'the abiding', 'the further shore', 'the unending', 'the bliss of effort', 'the supreme joy', 'the ineffable', 'the detachment', 'the holy city '.

The epithet 'Holy City' or 'City of Nibbāna' (*Nibbāna Nagara*) is of particular interest. The latter is found in Milinda's Questions and suggests a kind of fellowship.[22] It is also very significant that Dhamma, which is equated with *Nibbāna* in the Milinda Pañha[23] is called the 'Lord's City of Dhamma'.

Does this mean that there will be some sort of personal existence in the final state? To this question Buddhists refuse to give either an affirmative or a negative answer, because such answers would not be consistent with the Buddha's rejection of eternalism and nihilism. They prefer to leave the matter as a paradox.

But to many such paradoxes give neither consolation to the heart nor satisfaction to the mind. Some have therefore turned to upanishadic ideals of union with the Brahmā and call to their aid the *Tevijja Sutta*[24] where the Buddha speaks of the goal in terms of union with Brahmā as a result of the practice of universal love, or *Brahma Vihāras*. Incidentally, it may be noted that the Sanskrit term *Nirvāna* seems to have existed before the rise of Buddhism (as we could infer from the reference the Buddha makes to this term), and was used as a synonym for the Upanishadic ideal of *Moksha*. This notion of absorption into the Absolute, however, has been held to be a heretical view which has crept into Buddhism.

(c) Ethical immortality

G. C. Dev has made an interesting alternative suggestion. He says that while the Buddha denied immortality as a metaphysical concept, he accepted it as a moral achievement which *Nibbāna* as 'ethical immortality' signified. *Nibbāna* is thus 'the philosophy of permanence in Buddha's ethics'. Once *Nibbāna* is achieved, 'it remains for ever and ever and does not part company with us.'[25]

Dev explains the concept of ethical immortality as follows:

> Buddha's concept of Nirvāna is more akin to immortality as an achievement than as an ever-accomplished, metaphysical fact. When man becomes free from the bondage of desire, there is in him a stable consciousness of peace and this is not and cannot be touched by death. Immortality as an achievement means this. The differences between Nirvāna as enlightenment and Mahāpari-Nirvāna, death after enlightenment, possibly is this: even after enlightenment, while the body lasts as a physical process, there is a mind, a psychical process corresponding to it and there are ups and downs in it. But this cannot throw the enlightened man off his balance, because behind lies Nirvāna, the ever-soothing consciousness of infinite, unalloyed bliss. But when the body falls, its counterpart, the physical process, also ceases and the only thing that remains is the consciousness of Nirvāna. We cannot give it the name Buddha either. By Buddha, we mean a mind-body-complex of a particular type, the great struggler, the great seeker of truth, and the great benefactor of man, while Nirvāna precisely means the resulting achievement. This is what I presume Buddha means when he says that after his passing away, nothing temporal of him will remain. This cannot touch the eternal, ethical element that constitutes the essence of Nirvāna.[26]

According to this view, *Nibbāna* is an ethical achievement which has the quality of immortality. But who or what is it that achieves immortality? Can he or it be identified? Dev does not explain this clearly. Could the 'consciousness of *Nirvāna*' be explained in terms of *citta*?

(d) A state of personality (citta)

In *The Psychology of Nirvāna*, Rune Johansson advances an interpretation, on the basis of the Pali Nikāyas, of the term *citta* in which one finds a satisfactory concept of unity, identity and continuity of the 'empirical, functional self'. He describes *Nibbāna* as a state of personality but notes that 'human personality, contrary to what we generally read, does not consist in "personal factors" (*Khandha*), but rather in *citta* (generally translated mind)' which is defined as follows:

Citta is the core of personality, the centre of purposiveness, activity, continuity and emotionality. It is not a 'soul' (*attā*) but it is *the empirical functional* self. It is mainly conscious but not restricted to the momentary conscious contents and processes. On the contrary, it includes all the layers of consciousness, even the unconscious: by it the continuity and identity are safeguarded. It has a distinctly individual form.[27]

In this passage we have more than a hint that there is some form of personal existence after the death of the Arahat or Tathāgata. Referring to the conversation between Vacchagotta and the Buddha, quoted above, where the similes of fire and the ocean are used, he writes:

The idea must be that there is some sort of similarity between the ocean and an extinct fire, possibly the homogeneity, lack of differentiation and distinguishing traits, the 'calmness' and even distribution. Perhaps the fire was thought to 'go back' to some diluted, 'calm' existence, evenly distributed in matter, when it was extinguished (but without ceasing to be fire). In any case, the quotation proves that the Tathāgata was thought to continue existing in some form after death, as the ocean certainly exists.[28]

In this connection, Johansson discusses at some length the famous Udāna passage, 'there is a not-born, a not-become, a not-made . . .', noting that the key words in the text are adjectives, leaving the noun to be supplied. He advances the interpretation that the text refers to the personal *condition* of the *arahat* rather than to a metaphysical reality.

Here once again we see the necessity to smuggle in some idea of a soul in a disguised form, without which Buddhism seems to end in nihilism. But in trying to save Buddhism from nihilism Johansson borders on the opposite error of eternalism. Johansson is aware that his interpretation is not fully satisfactory. He modestly remarks: 'we have no illusion that this investigation is the final one of *Nibbāna*. But considering the many different explanations in contemporary literature every serious study should be helpful.'[29]

Perhaps we can do no better than leave the matter as a paradox. G. R. Welbon, after examining the various interpretations, inclines to the view of L. de la Vallée Poussin that probably *Nirvāna* signified 'un séjour inébranlable'[30] (an impregnable place of sojourn). He says:

> It need be neither cowardice nor ignorance that forces us to say finally that Nirvāna's 'meanings' are many and include both annihilation and bliss, negation and affirmation, non-existence and existence.[31]

From this discussion of the question of self-identity in Buddhism in relation to the doctrine of *anattā*, of karma and rebirth and of *nibbāna*, we see the interminable difficulties that have plagued Buddhist thought. The various solutions to the problem put forward tend either towards nihilism or eternalism. Is there a way out of this dilemma? Can we arrive at a concept of the self that can hold together both poles of nihilism and eternalism without one contradicting the other?

In the chapters that follow an attempt is made to see whether the Christian understanding of man can throw light on this matter. It is an attempt to use biblical perspectives in relation to the *tilakkhaṇa*,[32] particularly in relation to the doctrine of *anattā*, as a possible solution to the problem in a Buddhist-Christian context.

Theories about the self in general focus either on the *individual man*, his choices and self-awareness, or on the *social man*, his responses to and interrelatedness with other men. Buddhism is radically on the side of individualism. Christianity stresses the social nature of man. My suggestion is that a plausible solution to the problem of self-identity could be found in the biblical insight that the true self is to be found, not in the isolated individual, but in personal existence constituted by inter-personal relationships; not in the egocentric I, as the *anattā* doctrine stresses, but in the mutuality of the I and the Thou, which the term *pneumā* signifies. It is in the understanding of man as *anattā-pneuma* (non-egocentric relationality) that one should seek a solution to the problem of the self.

8 The Biblical View of Man

In any attempt to understand the Biblical view of man, it is of paramount importance, as A. R. Johnson says,

> to take note of the fact that Israelite thinking, like that of the so-called 'primitive' peoples of the present day, is predominantly synthetic. It is characterized in large measure by what has been called the grasping of totality. Phenomena are readily perceived as being in some kind of relationship; they are readily found to participate in some sort of whole. This recognition of the mental activity of the Israelites as predominantly synthetic, the awareness of totality, is important. It is, perhaps, hardly too much to say that it is the 'Open Sesame' which unlocks the secrets of the Hebrew language and reveals the riches of the Israelite mind.[1]

Biblical scholarship has established quite conclusively that there is no dichotomous concept of man in the Bible, such as is found in Greek and Hindu thought. The Biblical view of man is holistic, not dualistic. The notion of the soul as an immortal entity which enters the body at birth and leaves it at death is quite foreign to the biblical view of man. The biblical view is that man is a unity; he is a unity of soul, body, flesh, mind, etc., all together constituting the whole man. None of the constituent elements is capable of separating itself from the total structure and continuing to live after death The biblical view is that God created man entire, and in his entirety he must be saved (salvation means wholeness). The biblical message is concerned with the ultimate fulfilment of the total life of man.

It is therefore of paramount importance that at the outset of our investigation we make it quite clear that in the Bible there is no concept of an immortal soul as found in Greek and Hindu thought. On the contrary, there is much in common between the Buddhist and Biblical teachings about the self. However, this notion of an immortal soul is deeply embedded in popular Christian thinking and theologians are aware of the problems it has created for a true understanding of the teaching of the Bible. For this reason they strongly feel that this wrong notion must be rejected. It would suffice to quote two eminent theologians on this matter.

Karl Barth says that we must make an earnest protest against this non-biblical dualistic notion:

> We necessarily contradict the abstractly dualistic conception which so far we have summarily called Greek, but which unfortunately must also be described as the traditional Christian view. According to this view, soul and body are indeed connected, even essentially and necessarily united, but only as two 'parts' of human nature. . . .
>
> In general, the character and result of this anthropology are marked by a separation of the soul over the body, a humiliation of the body under the soul, in which both really become not merely abstractions but in fact two 'co-existing' figments – a picture in which probably no real man ever recognized himself, and with which one cannot possibly do justice to the biblical view and concept of man. It was disastrous that this picture of man could assert and maintain itself for so long as the Christian picture. We must earnestly protest that this is not the Christian picture.[2]

Paul Tillich calls the soul-theory a superstition which must be radically rejected:

> 'Immortality' in the sense of the Platonic doctrine of the immortality of the soul, was used very early in Christian theology, and in large sections of Protestant thought it has replaced the symbol of resurrection. In some Protestant countries it has become the last remnant of the whole Christian message, but it has done so in the non-Christian pseudo-Platonic form of the continuation of the temporal life of an individual after death without a body. Where the symbol of immortality is used to express this popular superstition, it has been radically rejected by Christianity; for participation in life eternal is not 'life hereafter'. Neither is it a natural quality of the soul. It is rather the creative act of God, who lets the temporal separate itself from and return to the eternal. It is understandable that Christian theologians who are aware of these difficulties reject the term 'immortality'

altogether, not only in its form in popular superstition but also in its genuine platonic form.[3]

Thus we see – and the investigation to follow will bear it out – that Buddhism and Christianity are one in rejecting the idea of a soul entity. In fact we could speak of a Christian doctrine of *anattā*, which in a sense is far more radical than the Buddhist doctrine and which does not fall into the error of either eternalism or nihilism. We could discover in the Bible a 'no' to eternalism and 'no' to nihilism, and a solution to the problem of the self in which the dialectical tension between these two extremes is brought into a synthesis by the concept of 'spirit'.

I do not propose to go into a detailed exposition of the biblical view of man, except to deal with the salient features in so far as they have a bearing on the problem with which we are concerned. There is a large literature dealing with the subject, as indicated in the footnotes. What follows is an attempt to restate the biblical teaching about man in the context of Buddhist thought.

2.   MAN AS CREATURE

(a) Man a mortal being
The biblical teaching about man is crystallised in one sentence of seven words: 'God created man in His own image.'[4] Two fundamental truths are implied in this sentence – that man is a creature, and that man bears the image of God.

To say that man is created is to say that he is a creature subject to mortality. Because man is created he can come to an end like anything else that has been created. The doctrine of creation is the biblical 'no' to eternalism (*sassata diṭṭhi*). This expresses the fundamental truth, that a created being has an element of non-being in him. Creatureliness implies non-being, with the natural necessity of death and the possibility of ultimate negation. This is implied in the doctrine of *Creatio ex nihilo* (*Creation out of nothing*).

Although, as a formula, *creatio ex nihilo* does not appear in the Bible, the idea is implicit in some passages. A striking passage is 2 Maccabees 7:28 – 'I beg you, child, look at the sky and the earth; see all that is in them and realize that God made them out of nothing, and that man comes into being in the same way' (N.E.B.) The idea is unmistakably expressed in Hebrews 11 : 3 – 'By faith we perceive that the universe was fashioned by the word of God, so that the visible came forth from the invisible' (N.E.B.). So also is the phrase in Romans 4:17 – 'God . . . who summons things that are not yet in existence as if they already were' (N.E.B.). It is possible that the priestly writer of the Genesis narrative, as C. A. Simpson argues, 'was endeavouring to present the idea of a *creatio ex nihilo*, at least in so far as he could conceive of it' in the opening words of the first chapter.[5]

This doctrine of *creatio ex nihilo* implies the impermanence (*anicca*) of all things apart from the Creator who maintains them by the power of His word in existence. As they were created out of nothing at His word, so they vanish into nothingness at His word. As all things, including man, have been created out of nothing, so all things, including man, stand *vis-à-vis* the threat of non-being (*anicca*).

The truth of man's creatureliness, of his anattahood, of his being threatened by non-being, which is implicit in the doctrine of *creatio ex nihilo*, is well stated by Karl Barth:

> Creaturely reality means reality on the basis of *creatio ex nihilo*, creation out of nothing. Where nothing exists – and not a kind of primal matter – then through God there has come into existence that which is distinct from Him. . . . Everything outside God is held constantly by God over nothingness. Creaturely nature means existence in time and space, existence with a beginning and end, existence that becomes, in order to pass away again. Once it was and once it will no longer be. . . . The creature is threatened by the possibility of nothingness and of destruction, which is excluded by God – and only by God. If a creature exists, it is only maintained in its mode of existence if God so wills. If He did not so will, nothingness would inevitably break from all sides. The creature itself could not rescue and preserve itself.[6]

Taking man himself as the paradigm of creaturely being, the characteristic of which is dependence and 'nullity', John Macquarrie also sees the importance of the doctrine of *creatio ex nihilo* as expressing the truth about man's creatureliness:

> The importance of the doctrine of *creatio ex nihilo* would seem to be that it draws attention to the fact that any particular being stands, so to speak, between nothing and Being. It is, insofar as it

participates in being, but any time it may cease to be. It both is and is not, for in order for anything to be something particular and determinate and recognizable as such, it is necessary that we should be able to say not only what it is but what it is not. This means in effect that negativity enters into the very way in which any particular being is constituted, or that nullity (nothingness) is an essential constituent of creaturehood. Again, man is the paradigmatic case, for we have seen that he actually experiences the 'nothingness' that enters into his existence. But this negativity, which in man can get raised to the level of explicit consciousness, is a universal characteristic of creaturely being.[7]

Recognition of this 'universal characteristic of creaturely being' corroborates the truth expressed by the doctrine of *anattā* and leaves no room at all for a notion of eternalism in the biblical view of man.

The biblical view of the unity of the self is a further protection against eternalism (*sassata diṭṭhi*). As has already been indicated, no trace of the body-soul dualism is found in the Bible. In Hebrew thought man is fundamentally a unity, a fact which needs to be stressed. As Ryder Smith says: 'a man without a body is not a man for the Hebrew. . . . The Platonic belief in the 'immortality of the soul' when it is once rid of the encumbrances of the body, is quite alien to the Hebrew mind.'[8] H. Wheeler Robinson, summing up the Old Testament teaching about man, says:

> The idea of human nature implies a unity, not a dualism. There is no contrast between body and soul, such as the words instinctively suggest to us. The shades of the dead in Sheol . . . are not called 'souls' or 'spirits' in the Old Testament; nor does the Old Testament contain any distinctive word for body, as it surely would have done, had this idea been sharply differentiated from that of the soul. Man's nature is a product of two factors – breath-soul, which is the principle of life, and the complex of physical organs which this animates. Nothing but a 'shade' remains which is neither body nor soul. . . . The Hebrew idea of personality is an animated body, not an incarnated soul.[9]

Thus we see that theologians and biblical scholars are in agreement that there is no notion of an immortal soul in the Bible. Let us now look at some significant biblical terms.

(b) Meaning of nephesh

The important word in our understanding of the Hebrew view of man is *nephesh*, which has been translated 'Soul' in old versions of the Bible. But this word is used simply to designate 'man' or indeed even 'animal' and has nothing to do with the idea of an immortal soul. Norman Snaith warns:

> Preachers need to realize that if they use Genesis 2 : 7 to refer to man's immortal soul, they must also assume, on the basis of Genesis 2 : 19 and of other passages also, that an animal also has an immortal soul.[10]

Nephesh cannot designate an immortal soul because at death the *nephesh* 'goes out'[11] i.e. it ceases to exist, lingering only so long as the body is a body.[12] 'There is nowhere a suggestion', says H. Wheeler Robinson, 'that the soul survives the man whose life it was; the inhabitants of the nether world (Sheol) are not souls but shades (*rephaim*).'[13] Thus the word *nephesh* is never used of a disembodied spirit or being after death. The inhabitants of Sheol are *rephaim*, a condition which cannot really be called life. It is, as S. B. Frost puts it, a state where 'nothing means anything any more.'[14] The Hebrews had no clear notion of what happens after death, although there were weak approaches to such a notion, but even in such approaches they could not think in terms of a disembodied soul.

It is possible that the need for some concept of life after death resulted in some compromise with the Greek notion of the soul in the inter-testamental literature. Thus, in the *Wisdom of Solomon*, there are more or less positive hints of the Greek notions of the pre-existence of the soul, the immortality of the soul and the idea that the soul goes to Hades. A well-known passage reads: 'The souls of the just are in God's hand, and torment shall not touch them. In the eyes of the foolish they seem to be dead. . . . But they are at peace . . . they have a sure hope of immortality.'[15]

In II Esdras 7 : 102–115 there is evidence of the belief that the souls will be preserved after death for judgement. But in this connection Ryder Smith has a very significant comment to make. He points out a fundamental difference between the Greek idea of the immortality of the soul and the view found in the Wisdom literature: 'For Plato the "souls" of all men, whether good or bad, are intrinsically immortal; in Wisdom immortality is confined to the good.' In *Sirach* and *Wisdom* God takes action in Hades, punishing the bad in it. 'The belief that he does nothing there is gone.'[16] This means that immortality does not, as in Greek thought, arise from the intrinsic nature of man but is essentially a gift of God. It is also significant that other apocryphal books, such as *Maccabees, Tobit, Judith* and in particular *Ecclesiasticus*, preserve the Hebrew usage of the term *nephesh* and do not under the pressure of necessity yield to the Greek notion. It is even more significant that in the New Testament the usage of *psychē* corresponds by and large to the Hebrew *nephesh*. This is an indication that the Greek notion of the soul, which had an influence on Wisdom literature, had no influence on the New Testament writings, as we shall presently see.

(c) Meaning of psychē

In the New Testament the term *psychē* continues to maintain the same unitary concept of man, following many of the usages of the Old Testament, although on occasion it perhaps somewhat in-dividualises it (*psychē*) as the centre of thoughts and feelings. But nowhere is the *psychē* conceived as existing in a bodiless state. The New Testament nowhere teaches the doctrine of the immortality of the soul of Platonic thought.

Like *nephesh*, *psychē* is used in the sense of 'life', 'vitality' or 'aliveness'. It is life that can be cared for, saved or lost, sought or laid down.[17] In Romans 11 : 3, Paul quotes the Septuagint of 1 Kings 19:10: '. . . and they seek my life' (*psychē*), where *psychē* clearly means 'life'. Romans 16 : 4 gives exactly the same meaning. This life is the natural aliveness or vitality which man shares with other living beings and is contrasted with the lifeless things which are called *apsychos*, a generic term for all inanimate objects.[18] This is only 'natural life' as distinct from 'spiritual life'.[19]

Psychē is also used in the psychological sense as the seat of feeling, thought and will. Thus the soul can be deeply grieved or exalted.[20] It can be addressed and complimented on its possessions.[21] *Psychē* is used reflexively in association with emotional feelings and as expressions of the will, such as desire or attitude or determination.[22]

There are a number of instances where *psychē* is used for an individual person or persons. A number of these are found in Acts. In Romans 2 : 9, Paul speaks of 'every soul of man that worketh evil', where not only is *psychē* used in the sense of 'person', but also as the agency of evil. This does not mean that the soul is one part of man that can sin; *psychē* is here used for the whole person as capable of sinning. In Romans 13 : 1 this same usage is repeated without a reference to sin. In 2 Cor. 12:15 Paul speaks of being 'spent for your souls', by which he means giving himself for them as persons. *Psychē* can also mean unity of persons when qualified with 'one'.[23]

It must be stressed that *psychē*, when used of the individual person, refers to the person as a whole and not an entity within him. It is thus the whole person who sins, not any part of him.[24] This wholeness or unity of the person is further emphasised in Paul's use of *psychē* in connection with *sōma*, which is an inclusive term for the total human being in its physical aspect.[25] Paul uses a series of terms in his anthropology, such as *sōma, sarx, nous, psychē* and *pneuma*, which only suggest the diversity of aspect within the intrinsic unity of man.

In two places there appears to be a derogatory view of the *psychē* (person), in Paul's use of *psychikos* to describe the 'natural' or 'unspiritual' as opposed to the spiritual man.[26]

On the other hand there are instances where *psychē* seems to receive a heightened meaning[27] and where the salvation of the *psychē* is also spoken of.[28] This could probably be explained by the fact that *psychē* often tends to be drawn into the meaning of *pneuma*. When a person is sanctified by the spirit it is the whole person (*psychē*) which is sanctified. The principle of unity is preserved in every instance. There is nothing in this usage to suggest that *psychē* is immortal.[29]

3.   INSTANCES SUGGESTIVE OF A DUALISM

There are however a few instances which seem to suggest a dichotomy or trichotomy. In this connection the verse most often quoted is Mat. 10:28, where Jesus says: 'Do not fear those who kill the body; rather fear him who can destroy both body and soul in hell.'[30] Oscar Cullmann's comment on this verse is as follows:

It might seem to presuppose the view that the soul has no need of the body, but the context of the passage shows that this is not the case. Jesus does not continue: 'Be afraid of him who kills the soul'; rather 'fear him who can slay both soul *and* body in Gehenna.' That is, fear God, who is able to give you over completely to death; to wit, when he does not resurrect you to life. We shall see, it is true that the soul is the starting-point of the resurrection, since, as we have said, it can hardly be possessed by the Holy Spirit in a way quite different from the body. The Holy

Spirit already lives in our inner man. 'By the Holy Spirit who dwells in you' (already), says Paul in Romans 8:11, 'God will also quicken your mortal bodies.' Therefore those who kill only the body are not to be feared. It can be raised from the dead. Moreover it must be raised. The soul cannot always remain without a body. And on the other side we hear in Jesus' saying in Mathew 10:28 that the soul can be killed. The soul is not immortal. There must be a resurrection for both; since the Fall the whole man is 'sown corruptible.' [31]

Referring to this verse J. Barr says:

> This is hardly a statement of the natural immortality of the disembodied soul, but means rather that the life of the self is a matter between man and God or man and devil.[32]

We must also remember that Jesus was a Jew, and His views about man were largely influenced by the Jewish thinking during His time.[33]

1 Thessalonians 5:23 is another verse often quoted in this connection: 'May your spirit and soul and body be preserved entire, without blame, at the coming of the Lord Jesus Christ.' W. D. Stacey comments on this verse as follows:

> The words *holoteles* and *holokleros* point to the real meaning. Paul is emphasizing the entirety of the preservation. The whole man is preserved, and spirit, and soul, and body, simply underline the inclusiveness of the conception. Man in every aspect, man in his wholeness, is to be preserved.[34]

Revelation 6:9 (cf. 20:4) also needs to be looked at. 'And when he had opened the fifth seal, I saw under the altar the souls of them that were slain for the word of God, and for the testimony which they held.' This picture is taken directly from the sacrificial ritual of the Temple where the blood of the sacrificial animal was offered at the foot of the altar. So the souls of the martyrs *'beneath the altar'* (mark the phrase) means the life-blood of the martyrs which has been poured out as an offering and a sacrifice to God.[35] It was the Hebrew belief that life was in the blood, so that Deuteronomy 12:23 and Leviticus 17:14 say that 'blood is the soul.' In this light the 'souls of the martyrs' means their life-blood shed at the altar.

Finally, we must note that there are a few passages where one could possibly trace some influence of the Greek idea of immortality. They are 2 Corinthians 5:1–5; Philippians 1:21–23 and 3:8–10. But it is significant that in these passages the word *psychē* does not occur at all.

These summary investigations lead to the conclusion that there is hardly any trace of the Greek idea of the soul in the Bible as a whole, and that in the New Testament in particular, the conception of man is based on the Hebraic notion of man as an intrinsic unity, with a diversity of aspects.[36]

4. PSYCHĒ-SARX AND NĀMA-RŪPA

The psycho-physical unity of man (or the psychosomatic unity, according to modern medical parlance), apart from God's spirit, can thus be analysed into soul (*psychē*) and flesh (*sarx*) and bears a close resemblance to the Buddhist *nāma-rūpa* analysis of man. *Psychē*, like *nāma*, corresponds to the psychical aspect of man in modern science and represents those processes which come within the field of psychology. *Sarx*, like *rūpa*, corresponds to physical processes with which biology is concerned. Just as in Buddhism man is unity of *nāma-rūpa*, so in the New Testament man is a unity of *psychē-sarx*; just as Buddhism says that there is no soul entity within the *nāma-rūpa* complex, so the Bible leaves no room for a notion of an immortal soul within the *psychē-sarx* unity of man.[37] Thus we could, in a sense, speak of a biblical doctrine of *anattā*. We could put the matter thus: psychosomatic creatureliness is *anattā* (i.e. soulless and substanceless).

There are three striking metaphors in the Bible with a Buddhist flavour which bear out the truth that creatureliness apart from the spirit of God is *anattā*.

Firstly there is the metaphor of dust.[38] The word 'dust' is a symbol for the fact that man bears the nature of created things. Just as created things perish, so man perishes: 'Dust thou art and to dust thou shalt return.'[39] 'All flesh is grass,' says Isaiah, 'and all its beauty is like the flower of the field. The grass withers and the flower fades.'[40] So is man. The Psalmist says: 'Man cannot abide in his pomp, he is like the beasts that perish.'[41]

Secondly, there is the metaphor of the shadow. Man is as empty as a shadow, says the Psalmist: 'Surely every man stands as a mere breath; surely man goes about as a shadow.'[42]

Thirdly, there is the metaphor of the *mist*. 'What is your life,' says St James, 'for you are a mist that appears for a little time and then vanishes.'[43] The Greek word *atmis* used here could mean vapour (KJV) or mist (RSV) or smoke. J. B. Phillips' translation reads: "What after all is your life? It is like a puff of smoke visible for a little while and then dissolving into thin air."

Not only would Christianity deny an ego-entity but also exclusive individuality, so that it could be said that the person (*puggala*), thought of in purely individualistic terms in his singularity and independence, does not in reality exist and cannot exist. If such a state were possible it could be described by the metaphors, *dust, shadow* and *mist*.[44]

In a sense, therefore, Christianity goes beyond Buddhism in its doctrine of *anattā* for two reasons.

Firstly, Buddhism, while denying the self, teaches that man has by a natural right moral capacity or sufficiency by which he is able to determine his own destiny; he has an intrinsic capability to work out his own salvation. Buddhism denies the self, but says that man must rely upon himself alone for 'salvation'. He is his own saviour.[45] Self-dependence and self-effort are the two keynotes of Buddhist ethics. In effect Buddhism says, 'Man is nothing (*anattā*) but man alone can do something to save himself.' In contrast Christianity could say: 'Man is nothing by himself and can do nothing to save himself.' It is by grace that man is saved and not by self-effort.

Secondly, the Buddhist theory of *karma* and rebirth implies that there is 'something' within man, either his *karma* or an operative mental or psychic force (*viññāṇa*) which has the power to cause or perpetuate life after death in 'persons' or momentary 'selves'. The Bible leaves no room for such a belief. Man has no power within himself to generate a life beyond the grave; he has no inherent right to immortality as Greek thought supposed. It is only by the power of God that man can inherit eternal life. He can do nothing to merit eternal life.

Thus in the Bible we have a thoroughgoing doctrine of *anattā* which in a sense is far more radical than the Buddhist doctrine. Thus when the Bible says 'no' to eternalism it says so without any reserve. Is the biblical view then a thorough-going nihilism?

5.   MAN AS IMAGE OF GOD

(a) The meaning of ruach (spirit)

The doctrine of man's creatureliness is the biblical stand against eternalism. Left at that the teaching of the Bible about man will fall nowhere short of nihilism. But the Bible takes the stand against nihilism too in its doctrine that man is created *in the image of God*. These few words define firstly, the nature of man as a creature and secondly, the relation between man and God. When the stress is on the word *created* (made) it indicates man's creatureliness; when the stress is on the word *image*, it indicates a relationship between God and man. This relationship, as Kraemer says, is a partnership: 'God gives to this being a commission, a mandate, that is: He speaks to him, He treats him as a partner, nothing more, nothing less.'[46] The image lies not in the human structure, but in the direct and positive relation of community between man and God.

Lesslie Newbigin brings out the meaning of *imago dei* with a striking illustration:

> The image of the king's head on a coin is part of the coin, and cannot be separated from it. Even if the king dies, the image remains on the coin. But there is another kind of image. On a still and cloudless night we may see the image of the moon in the water of a lake. So long as the water is unruffled by the wind, and the moon is not covered by cloud, the image will shine out – clear and beautiful. But if the cloud comes between the moon and the earth the image will disappear, or if the water is ruffled by wind the image will be scattered and distorted. Thus the image of the moon in the water does not belong to the water just in the same way that the image of the king on the coin belongs to the coin. The image depends upon a certain relationship between the moon and water. If this relationship is broken, the image is distorted.[47]

The Old Testament word that indicates the nature of this relationship is *ruach*. Reinhold Niebuhr says that *ruach* gradually becomes 'the more specific designation of man's relation to God, in distinction to *nephesh* which achieves a connotation identical with soul or *psychē*, or the life principle in man.'[48]

Ruach is God-given and never man-produced. As Norman Snaith says: 'A man can control his *nephesh* but it is the *ruach* which controls him.'[49] *Ruach* does not in any sense suggest man's oneness or identity with God, as in Hindu thought. The Bible is emphatic on the fact that God is Spirit and man is flesh, as the narrative of Genesis 6: 1 – 4 clearly shows. Man can live only if God gives him life. If God were to withdraw his spirit he dies; if he sends his spirit man lives.[50] Man is not naturally immortal. The Wisdom of Solomon has a verse which throws light on this matter:

> For God created man to be immortal and made him to be the image of his own eternity. Neverthless, through envy of the devil came death into the world; and they that do hold of his side do find it.[51]

This makes it clear that man is not made immortal but is made to be immortal. This he could gain only in a relationship with the Eternal. But this relationship has been distorted and blunted by the Fall. Immortality is not a natural possession of man. Man is not inherently, natively immortal. God alone is Eternal and it is only in relation to the Eternal that man can be eternal. The terms *image* and *ruach* mean the possibility of fulfilment in actuality, what is beyond human potentiality through a relation to the Eternal (the *Amata*).

Though man is *anattā*, he is able to ask the question about his destiny, analyse his nature as non-being and evaluate the flux in which he is involved, and thereby transcend himself. If man is aware of his nothingness (*anattā*) he must be something more than nothing. Man transcends his anattahood by questioning his very nature of non-being. In other words, there is a transcendental quality in man which enables him to rise above his finite existence. But this transcendental quality is not a natural property of the human structure as such. It cannot be identified with the power of *karma* or the power of the mind. If it were so it would nullify our insistence on *anattā*. If *anattā* is understood in its final depth, this transcendental quality cannot be found in man himself or derived from existence itself.

This transcendental quality is something that appears in the human structures, but transcends it in quality and power. The image of God appears in the human structure but is not its product. It transcends man. Man is not self-possessed from within as the doctrine of becoming implies, but is possessed from above. The image of God means the possession from above overcoming self-possession from below. This thought is contained in the significant New Testament term *pneuma*.

(b) The meaning of pneuma

W. D. Stacey distinguishes six senses of *pneuma* in the Pauline corpus: *Pneuma* (1) as applied to the Divine – to God, to the Holy Spirit and to the Spirit of Christ; (2) as a divine influence in the life of believers, creating in them 'spiritual gifts'; (3) as applied to 'seducing spirits' in opposition to the Divine Spirit; (4) as the evil influence which ensued from the disobedient spirits; (5) as a purely Christian spirit created in the believer which enables him to hold communion with God because spirit with spirit can meet; (6) as 'the natural possession of every man, which of itself is neither good nor bad, and is not easily distinguished from *psyche*.'[52] Of these six the three that are of immediate relevance to our investigation are the first and the last two, and a clear understanding of the relationship of one to the other is of very great importance in view of the common misconception prevailing in Christian thinking. On this matter Stacey writes with great clarity:

> It is with the spirit of man (sense 5) that God's Spirit is largely concerned, and here a word of warning is necessary. The relationship does not involve a confusion between the Holy Spirit and man. The Spirit (sense 1) is the key to the understanding of man's spirit (sense 5), but does not shade off into the other. In 1 Cor. 2:11 the Spirit of God is contrasted with the spirit of man in order to show the inadequacy of the latter. This, it is true, only reveals that there is no room for confusion between God and the natural spirit of man (sense 6). . . . THE SPIRIT OF MAN WAS ENERGIZED BY THE SPIRIT, BUT THE HUMAN SPIRIT NEVER ROSE TO SHARE THE DIVINE NATURE. THERE IS FELLOWSHIP AND COMMUNION, BUT NOT ABSORPTION . . . *Pneuma*, as an ordinary element in man, has little connection with the spirit of God, and a different approach will be needed there.[53]

To speak of personal *pneuma* as a natural possession of man (sense 6) could lead to a notion of the immortality of the spirit. Stacey warns us against such a misconception which might be deduced from 1 Cor. 5:5 and stresses that the natural spirit is mortal, morally indifferent and liable to corruption.[54] We could therefore say that the natural *pneuma* is no other than *psyche*; yet there is a difference.

Like *nephesh* and *psychē*, *pneuma* connotes the sense of vitality of life, but it has a distinctive meaning too. *Psychē* is used in the sense of 'aliveness' and it is that which distinguishes man from lifeless objects. The flute and harp are different from man because they are *apsychē* (lifeless).[55] *Psychē* life is the life man shares with the animals. But there is a life which man only can live. That life is '*pneuma*' and not '*psychē*'. This contrast is seen in the following verse: 'Thus it is written, 'the first Adam became a living being (*psychē*), the last Adam became a life-giving spirit (*pneuma*).'[56] While *psychē* expresses the life separated from God, *pneuma* expresses life derived from God. St Paul calls this separated self 'the carnal self',[57] as opposed to the spiritual self. In so far as the self is estranged from God, it becomes carnally minded and the end is death: 'To set one's mind on the flesh is death.' In so far as the self is genuinely related to God it is spiritually minded and becomes the true self. 'To set one's mind on the spirit is life and peace.'

While *psychē* and *pneuma* are thus opposed to one another, in some passages they are interrelated.[58] The idea is that the *psychē* is transformed by the *pneuma* into God-likeness, or into the image of God in Christ: 'And we all, with unveiled face, beholding the glory of the Lord, are being changed into His likeness from one degree of glory to another; for this comes from the Lord who is the Spirit.'[59] We could say that *pneuma* is *psychē* – the indivisible whole – raised to a new dimension of being by the power of the Spirit.

This brings us to a very important conclusion in our understanding of the nature of man. In highest spiritual dimension man is a creature with the possibility of non-being, and in his lowest degree of natural life he is a creature in the 'image of God'. Man is a unity of creatureliness and God-likeness; in other words, a unity of *anattā* and *pneuma*. The nature of man can thus be described as *anattā-pneuma*. *Anattā* indicates man's organic nature; the fact that within the psycho-physical organism there is no permanent immortal entity and that, as such, man is subject to *dukkha* and *anicca*. *Pneuma* indicates that extra dimension of being which makes man more than just a physical organism or a psychosomatic complex. *Pneuma* is not another substance or a thing (the 'thinking thing', *res cogita*); it is rather the dynamic quality which makes man a person. *Anattā-pneuma* signifies the self-empty but spirit-full life.

9 Man as 'Spirit' – Pneuma

1. THE DIMENSIONS OF THE 'SPIRIT'

(a) Multidimensional unity of the self

We ended the last chapter with a brief consideration of the meaning of spirit in the New Testament, and its significance for an understanding of the true nature of man. Since this is a key concept, we need to go deeper and consider further its theological implications.

The New Testament term 'spirit' (*pneuma*), as has been indicated, is a term that has to do with the individual man when used descriptively as a concept of the authentic self; it has also to do with the Divine Spirit as the ground of being and the Power that creates community and posits the self. (Note the simple 's' in reference to man and the capital 'S' in reference to the Divine Spirit.) Without an understanding of spirit as a dimension of life it is not possible to understand the Divine Spirit and His relation to the human spirit. Thus Tillich observes that:

> A new understanding of the term 'spirit' as a dimension of life is a theological necessity. . . . It is quite probable that the fading of the symbol 'Holy Spirit' from the living consciousness of Christianity is at least partly caused by the disappearance of the word 'spirit' from the doctrine of man. Without knowing what spirit is, one cannot know what Spirit is.[1]

The concept of spirit rightly understood, as we shall see, provides a notion of self-identity which is neither the entity in substance philosophy, nor a 'nonentity' which characterises a process philosophy but contains within itself what is true and needful in both positions.

To begin with, a word needs to be said about the meaning of the word 'dimension'. Here I follow Tillich closely in using this term 'dimension' as a description of the various forms of life which, while preserving distinction, maintains a unity without contradiction. This is preferable to the description of life in terms of levels, that is, the hierarchical distinction of degrees of life beginning with the inorganic and ascending to the divine life. Such a view tends to isolate the different forms of life as contradistinctive levels, which ultimately leads to a dualism. This idea of levels seems to be behind the Buddhist argument that the infant is one thing, the young boy another, and the grown up quite another; just as the flame of the first watch is not the same as the flame of the middle, and the flame of the middle watch not the same as the flame of the third watch. Of course there is a continuity of *dhammas* (*dhamma santati*) but 'one uprises, another ceases; it runs on as though there were no before, no after; consequently neither the one (*dhamma*) nor another is reckoned as the last consciousness.'[2] Although the *dhamma santati* idea has some likeness to the idea of dimensions, it is different in that theoretically the 'after' does not contain the 'before'. But 'dimension' is a comprehensive term for the unity and diversity of life which embraces the inorganic, including the realms of the macro-cosmic and the micro-cosmic, and the organic, which includes the realms of the plant, the animal, the human and the spiritual beings. They all form a multidimensional unity of life. Spirit is thus all-inclusive as a totality in which the whole contains all the parts in distinction and unity.

(b) Spirit as all-inclusive totality

Spirit is the reality immanent in all creation, comprehending all things and all realms multidimensionally in an all-inclusive totality. This thought is in line with the Hebrew conception of the Spirit of God immanent and active in creation and in human life. God as Spirit is everywhere and always present in the universe as the inner final reality of all things. Spirit is, as Teilhard de Chardin says, 'the within of things'; the within of things as their purposive and directive power, the power immanent in the process of evolution. Such an understanding is necessary to make sense of the process of evolution. Up to a point the theory of evolution is right in maintaining that creation has been and is accomplished by the agency of energies which are intrinsic in evolving matter, but this theory fails to explain how those energies originate and what guides and controls them. The understanding of Spirit as the immanent reality suggests a solution to this problem. Such an understanding also gives us an insight into the nature of Incarnation. Because the

Spirit of God is present in everything the Incarnation seems more reasonable. We can therefore speak of Christ as the within of all things for 'in Him everything in heaven and earth was created.'[3] Thus, to link up the Holy Spirit with the immanence of God in His creative activity, and the Incarnation of Christ in His redemptive work, is to link up creation and redemption with the whole process of evolution, which is now seen as the one great increasing purpose of the Creator. We also see here the principle in which 'all things hold together'[4] or cohere.

Spirit is the principle of coherence in which the One and the many meet inherently in an all-inclusive totality, but which provides the power of genuine distinction. Spirit can cohere in all things in such a way as to be the *all-inclusive total ultimate reality*, and at the same time Spirit can be present in creation as the inner identity or the within of things within all distinctions that make for personal life and communal relationships. The nature of Spirit in one dimension is to be Unconditioned, Unmade, Unborn, Non-becoming as a distinctive eternal and ultimate principle and as such characterises the absolute Reality of substance philosophy. But Spirit in another dimension can inhere in the conditioned, the made, the born and the becoming as the creative power of identity and distinction underlying the unity and continuity of the process, and as such characterises the all-inclusiveness of process philosophies. In Spirit the genuineness of distinction and the all-inclusiveness of process cohere multidimensionally. Thus Spirit is a reality and power that is *immanent* and *eminent* at the same time. As an *immanent* reality Spirit allows identity and distinction through co-inherence, and as an *Eminent* Reality Spirit is all-inclusive as a total identity.

This does not, however, mean that spirit in man is an ephemeral form of the Divine Spirit, like a wave or bubble on the ocean. In the words of Oliver Quick, Spirit 'represents an invasive, rather than pervasive power'.[5] This is a point to which I shall return later for further clarification.

(c) Spirit as constituting personality

Spirit is the power of life that constitutes personality. Throughout the Bible it is maintained that God is the source of life, and, as religious thought developed, 'Spirit' as the breath of God came to be associated with the life created by God, particularly with human life. 'Spirit' as breath carries with it the idea of God's dynamic creative activity manifest particularly in persons. However, Spirit as the power of life is not identical with any substratum or separate entity within man, nor is it anything added to the organic structure which is animated by it. Spirit is rather the power of animation itself. It does not create a 'soul' in the individual; it is not a part added to the organic system; it cannot be located in the individual. Spirit is the dimension in which personality actualises itself, not as a separate entity, but as an identity within a unity. This personal aspect can never be understood apart from the relationship in which the self exists. In somewhat paradoxical terms, Kierkegaard tries to explain the nature of the self as spirit, and its relationship to Spirit as follows:

> Man is spirit. But what is spirit? Spirit is the self. But what is the self? The self is a relation which relates itself to its own self, or it is that in the relation (which accounts for it) that the relation relates itself to its own self; the self is not the relation (but consists in the fact) that the relation relates itself to its own self.[6]

Kierkegaard goes on to explain that this relation is a relation 'derived' and 'constituted' by virtue of a 'third term', the term of its relation to the ground of being. 'By relating itself to its own self and by willing to be itself, the self is grounded transparently in the power which posited it.'[7]

Thus we could say that man is spirit, spirit is the self, the self is a relation, and the ground of the relation is the Divine Spirit. Thus the self can never be understood in abstraction. It can only be understood in its dimension of which Spirit is the ground.

(d) Spirit as 'communal'

Spirit is the communal dimension of life in which a person as a person emerges in community. The self-integration of a person as a person happens in the encounter of person with person and in no other way. We cannot imagine a personal being as an entity made up of the five aggregates living outside a community of persons. If this is possible at all it will be an organism and not a person. Personal life cannot be actualised apart from a community, and likewise no community can come into being apart from personal life. Neither is actual apart from the other.

In the New Testament the Holy Spirit is in a very special manner the spirit of the 'community'. Spirit is the dimension of life of the Church as the body of Christ;[8] the source of its unity[9] and the fellowship in which the Jew and the Gentile find communion in God. The life of the Church consists in the participation of persons in the Spirit.[10] The Holy Spirit is the Spirit of fellowship which brings individuals out of their isolation into a community, making 'one body' of them. The basic truth is that the self is not an isolated individual but a *person*, the personal existence being found only in the relation of persons constituted by the Spirit.

In his book *Persons in Relation*, John Macmurray has convincingly set out the view that 'the self' is constituted by its relation to the Other; that it has its being in its relationships; and that this relationship is necessarily personal.[11] This personal existence of the self constituted by the relation of persons begins where all human life begins, with infancy. The infant is born into a love-relationship which is inherently personal. He differs from young animals of all kinds because of his total helplessness and dependence on the mother or those who care for him.[12] Although the infant cannot think for himself or do anything for himself, his behaviour is purposive and not merely instinctive or biological because he has, as Macmurray says, the capacity to express his feelings which presuppose a shared and co-operative existence:

> The baby's adaptation to his 'environment' consists in his capacity to express his feelings of comfort or discomfort; of satisfaction and dissatisfaction with his condition. Discomfort he expresses by crying; comfort by gurgling and chuckling, and very soon by smiling and crowing. The infant's cry is a call for help to the mother, an intimation that he needs to be cared for. . . . His expression of physical satisfaction is closely associated with being cared for, with being nursed, with the physical presence of the mother, and particularly with physical contact. . . . This is evidence that the infant has a need which is not simply biological but personal, a need to be in touch with the mother, and in conscious perceptual relation with her. And it is astonishing at what an early age a baby cries not because of any physiological distress, but because he has noticed that he is alone, and is upset by his mother's absence. Then the mere appearance of the mother, or the sound of her voice, is enough to remove distress and turn his cries into smiles of satisfaction. . . . All the infant's activities in maintaining his existence are shared and co-operative . . . the activities of an infant, taken as a whole, have a personal and not an organic form. They are not merely

motivated, but their motivation is governed by intention.[13]

Thus the mother-child relationship is the starting-point of personal life, and in the infant's purposeful behaviour which presupposes intention and motivation are to be found the germs of personal-communal development. About this personal-communal develop-ment or inter-personal relationship Macmurray writes:

> Personality is mutual in its very being. The self is one term in a relation between two selves. It cannot be prior to that relation and equally, of course, the relation cannot be prior to it. 'I' exist only as one member of the *'you and I'*. The self only exists in the communion of selves.[14]

(e) Spirit as the category of self-transcendence

In the personal-communal relationship, a person reaches beyond himself to the Other with whom he is related. In thus reaching out he transcends himself. Spirit is thus the category of self-transcendence. Man cannot lift himself above the conflicts and ambiguities of life. It is the Spirit which grasps him and lifts him into a transcendental unity. It is only in and through the Spirit that the self can go beyond the self as self. The main characteristic of the Spirit can be described as 'procession'. He is 'the Spirit of truth, who proceeds (*ekporeuetai*) from the Father'.[15] The man who has the Spirit is one who goes out of himself and beyond himself, being driven away by the Spirit. The Spirit is the Unconditioned in the conditioned, driving the conditioned beyond itself; it is the Uncreated in the created, grasping and drawing the created out of itself. Thus, as Tillich puts it:

> The 'in' of the divine Spirit is an 'out' for the human spirit. The spirit, a dimension of finite life, is driven into successful self-transcendence; it is grasped by something ultimate and uncon-ditional. It is still the human spirit; it remains what it is, but at the same time it goes out of itself under the impact of the divine Spirit.[16]

This self-transcendence is what existentialist philosophers call 'existence' in the sense of 'ex-sisting' or 'standing out'. This is the essential characteristic of spirit. To bring out the dynamic character of spirit as ex-sistence John Macquarrie has coined a new word *exience*, meaning 'going out'. He points out that 'the word "ex-ience" is formed in analogy with "transience" from Latin *ire*, to go.'[17]

The self, as spirit, transcends not only his body, not only his mind, but his very self, that is, the differentiated self. In transcending oneself one ceases to be an ego entity. But self-hood is always being fulfilled by being transcended. It is by transcending the self that the ego is negated and the authentic self is affirmed. Such transcendence is possible because the self exists only in relation to the Other and it is only in a personal-communal structure that the identity of the self is to be found. We need to go deeper into this aspect of the matter, at the risk of repetition, since it is basic to our understanding.

2. THE PERSONAL-COMMUNAL STRUCTURE OF 'SPIRIT'

(a) Individualisation and participation

In our search for a satisfactory concept of identity and continuity of the self which steers clear of the extremes of eternalism and nihilism, we fall into great difficulties, if we seek to solve the problem from a purely individualistic standpoint. The problem of man cannot be solved, as we have stressed, if man is treated as an individual, solitary being. The solution to the problem should be sought within the framework of the personal-communal nature of the self, in which the self emerges as a recognisable identity. This, we have argued, is the biblical point of view. As Tillich puts it, the self individualises itself as a 'person' in participation.

> When individualization reaches the perfect form which we call a 'person', participation reaches the perfect form which we call 'communion'. Man participates in all levels of life, but he participates fully only in that level of life which he is himself – he has communion only with persons. Communion is participation in another completely centred and completely individual self. In this sense communion is not something an individual might or might not have. Participation is essential for the individual, not accidental.
>
> No individual exists without participation, and no personal being exists without communal being. The person as a fully developed individual self is impossible without other fully developed selves. If he did not meet the resistance of other selves,

every self would try to make himself absolute. But the resistance of the other selves is unconditional. One individual can conquer the entire world of objects, but he cannot conquer another person without destroying him as a person. The individual discovers himself through this resistance. If he does not want to destroy the other person, he must enter into communion with him. In resistance of the other person the person is born. Therefore, there is no person without an encounter with other persons. Persons can grow only in the communion of personal encounter. Individualization and participation are interdependent on all levels of being.[18]

Probably no one expresses this point better than Martin Buber, to whom many theologians, including Tillich, are greatly indebted. Buber stresses not only that authentic being is found in participation, but that in this relationship one goes beyond oneself. He says:

> The fundamental fact of human existence is neither the individual as such nor the aggregate as such. Each considered by itself is a mighty abstraction. The individual is a fact of existence in so far as he steps into a living relation with other individuals. The aggregate is a fact of existence in so far as it is built up of living units of relations. The fundamental fact of human existence is man with man. What is peculiarly characteristic of the human world is above all that something takes place between one being and another, the like of which can be found nowhere in nature. Language is only a sign and a means for it; all achievement of the spirit has been incited by it. Man is made man by it; but on its way it does not merely unfold, it also decays and withers away. It is rooted in one being turning to another as another, as this particular other being, in order to communicate with it in a sphere which is common to them but which reaches out beyond the special sphere of each. I call this sphere, which is established with the existence of man as man but which is conceptually still uncomprehended, the sphere of 'betweens'. Though being realized in very different degrees, it is a primal category of human reality. This is where the genuine third alternative must begin.[19]

Buber's remark that the aggregate is 'built up of living units of relation' is very significant. He is using the word 'aggregate' in the sense of an individual built up of mental and physical factors. If we consider the five factors which make up the individual, as explained in Buddhism, we see that they are in a sense units of relation. Feelings, perceptions, ideations, and thoughts cannot arise independently and in isolation. There must be some interaction for them to arise. Similarly, *sarx, psychē, sōma, pneuma* etc. are what we may call relational terms. They indicate the truth that man is a 'communal' being in his very nature and constitution. He is created in the image of God; he is marked out for a special relationship and destiny. Man is not shut up or closed in his being. From the beginning to the end man is a 'communal' being. 'For we do not begin', writes W. E. Hocking, 'as solitary beings and then acquire community; we begin as social products and acquire the arts of solitude.'[20] Thus we could say with Buber: 'In the beginning is relation.'[21] Heidegger's philosophy rests on the realisation that 'all existence is co-existence'. 'The world is what I share with others.'[22] The 'I' is co-efficient with the 'Thou'. To be is to be related.

(b) The authentic self

This leads us to the important perception that it is in relationship that man finds his authentic being. 'Human personality,' says Ebner, 'always consists in the existence of the I in relation to the thou.'[23] Or as Buber puts it: 'Man is neither organic nor rational, but dialogic, that is, man becomes the authentic being only in a living relation with other individuals'; and further, 'I came into being over against the thou: all life is of the nature of encounter.'[24] All existence is co-existence. 'One cannot be without inter-being.'[25]

One of the essential marks of the authentic self is self-awareness. This means being separated from everything else in such a way as being able to look at everything else objectively. But in looking at everything else objectively, the self becomes aware of itself as related either positively or negatively to that which it looks at. Self-awareness is a simultaneous experience of self-relatedness.

To sum up: the meaning and significance of life is known and the fullness and depth of life is achieved in our relationships. Personality exists and grows only in the communion of personal encounter; it has a reality only in communion with other beings. Personality is never absorbed and lost in communion, and it can never be abstracted from communion without the peril of being completely lost. Personality is the identity of the self in the mutuality of the 'I' and the 'Thou': it is the identity of the self shining through the contingencies of community. Thus the authentic self or personality is not in the first instance something which we find in man as an isolated individual but something which we find in a relationship. Thus, logically, it is possible for one to lose oneself and become *anattā* in the nihilistic sense of the word, if one could sever all relationships. But on the other hand, one could lose oneself without annihilating the self in a relationship which takes one beyond oneself. This in essence is the biblical understanding of the 'communal' dimension of *pneuma*.

3. IS SPIRIT ANOTHER DISGUISED SOUL-THEORY?

The question may yet be asked: Is the idea of spirit, as the principle of life which constitutes personality and creates self-identity, another soul-theory in disguise? In effect, are we not speaking of the immortality of the person (*puggala*) though not of the immortality of the soul?

In discussing the biblical meaning of spirit it was stressed that no concept of immortality could be deduced from this term as used in the Bible. John Macquarrie, summing up this aspect of the meaning of spirit, also stresses that spirit cannot be thought of as some kind of substance:

> What then do we mean by 'spirit' when we apply the term to the being of man? We have already seen that the word is meant to indicate that extra dimension of being which belongs to man and makes him more than just a physical organism or an unusually complex animal. We need not suppose that spirit is some kind of substance. To reify spirit is to commit an error in categorization and even tends to reduce spirit to the level of that very thinghood, beyond which the symbol of spirit was meant to point us in the first place. But the dominance of things, both in our thinking and our language, is so great that we tend to conceive whatever it is about which we think or talk on the analogy of another thing. Thus modern Western thought has tended to follow Descartes in regarding spirit as *res cogitans*, the 'thinking thing'. Spirit is not another thing or substance. It belongs in a different category. It is rather a dynamic form, a quality of being that differentiates man (and whatever other spiritual beings may exist) from animals, plants, sticks, and stones.[26]

We may restate this point by contrasting the concept of spirit in the Bible with the concept of the soul in substance philosophy.

In the first place, according to substance philosophies, the soul is man's natural possession; it belongs to him and is inseparable from him. In contrast, the spirit in man which makes him an authentic person is not his by a natural right; it is not what man merits or attains to or achieves. The spirit is not *a priori* in man. It is given. As Karl Barth has put it:

> Man *has* spirit. By putting it this way we describe spirit as something that comes to man, something not essentially his own but to be received and actually received by him, something that totally limits his constitution and thus totally determines it.[27]

When we say that man *has* spirit we do not describe a property of man, a kind of element in his constitution which he has by natural right. Spirit is a 'gift'. 'Man "has" the Spirit but it cannot be said that he is spirit.'[28]

Secondly, in substance philosophies the soul is considered to be immortal and indestructible. But the Spirit which elevates man's spirit to the Divine can be withdrawn and man can cease to be.[29] Spirit is not a divine spark in man which is of the very essence of the Divine, as Barth makes clear:

> It is not that man, having Spirit, is of divine essence even if only in a part or in the core of his being. On the contrary, the creatureliness of the whole man cannot be more evident than in the fact that he stands in need of this 'may', of this freedom to live which is not immanent in him but comes from without.[30]

Barth uses the striking illustration of the circle and the mathematical centre: 'The Spirit is in man and belongs to him as the mathematical centre is in and belongs to the circle.'[31] Without the circle there can be no centre. 'The whole man is of the Spirit, since the Spirit is the principle and power of the life of the whole man.'[32]

This must not be confused with the Hindu *Advaita* view, that like a wave or a bubble on the ocean a person is ephemeral in himself, yet, like a wave or a bubble he is a temporary form assumed of Something abiding – the very stuff of the Ocean. He is not a 'Thou' which is identical with the 'That'. This point will be further dealt with later.

Thirdly, the soul in substance philosophies is an independent reality, having the power to be within itself. But the finite self as spirit is qualified by its relation to Spirit and is dependent on that relationship. The finite spirit is dependent for its self-actualisation and self-transcendence on its participation with the Divine Spirit.

About this relation Barth says:

　Spirit is thus the principle of man's relation to God, of man's fellowship with Him. This relation and fellowship cannot proceed from man himself, for God is his Creator and he His creature. He himself cannot be its principle. If this is indeed possible for him, and if he on his side realises it as movement from him towards God, this is because the movement of God towards him has preceded and because he may in his movement imitate it.[33]

About the divine-human relationship Barth goes on to say:

　The biblical statements about the Spirit as the principle of the existence of man in the covenant of grace are related to those about the Spirit as the principle of his creatureliness in such a way that the former include the latter as a presupposition, in so far as the latter show and explain how man (together with the beasts) already stands as a creature under the same judgement and what will be his being as partner of the covenant of grace; as promise in so far as man has a certain hope in and for his creatureliness – the hope which in the New Testament is described as the resurrection of the dead, the resurrection of the whole man.[34]

Thus it is clearly seen that the biblical understanding of *pneuma* leaves no room at all for a concept of an immortal soul.

4. THE ANATTĀ-PNEUMA CONCEPT

We have now arrived at a stage when we could bring the distinctive Buddhist concept of *anattā* and the distinctive Christian concept of *pneuma* together, and see how they are interrelated. The yoking of these two concepts together opens up new dimensions of our understanding of the meaning of personhood, which could facilitate inter-religious and inter-cultural dialogue. There are three dimensions in which we could see the mutual relation of these two concepts, each enriching, deepening and filling up the gaps in the other. They are not exclusive dimensions; they merge with one another.

There is firstly the psycho-physical or *nāma-rūpa* dimension. Here *anattā* means the rejection of *atta* or an eternal self or soul. Buddhism is unique in its rejection of any permanent entity within man, and this is a corrective to the wrong notion that has invaded popular Christian thinking. Christian theology can be greatly enriched by the absorption of the *anattā* doctrine into its system of thought. However, the *pañcakkhandha* analysis seems to reduce man to a psychosomatic organism. But *pneuma* points to a dimension of reality which cannot be exhausted by a scientific or psychological analysis of finite life; it signifies that extra dimension of finite life which is constitutive of authentic being which makes a person more than a bundle of aggregates or merely a psycho-physical organism or an unusually complex animal. *Pneuma* is not some kind of 'thing' or a substance parallel to the substance of physical entities; it is a dynamic quality of being which lifts man above finite existence.

There is secondly the ethico-social dimension. Ethically *anattā* means non-attachment, particularly to the false notion of the self or soul, which is the root cause of all evil. Relinquishing self, abolishing self is therefore the primary concern in Buddhism. It is the concern of every religion, but Buddhism stands unique in its ethical discipline designed to root out everything that inflames the self. But, overstressing non-attachment from a purely individualistic point of view can lead to isolation and a socially irrelevant ethic. *Pneuma* affirms this social dimension. It signifies the fact that to be is to be related; 'all existence is co-existence.' Man is therefore a socially responsible being. Authentic being is not what one attains for oneself, but something that is shared; something that brings persons into relationships with one another. Love is the basis of this shared life. It is love alone that is capable of uniting persons in such a way as to negate exclusive individuality and to complete and fulfil personality. But if one is not disciplined in non-attachment and forgets the ideal of self-obliteration, one will turn love and inter-personal relationship into a selfish game. Therefore *anattā*, with its stress on non-attachment will always be a safeguard against such a danger.

There is thirdly the transcendental dimension. *Anattā* implies the realisation of emptiness; the fully realised man is totally emptied of self. That realisation is *Nirvāna*. It is an experience in which self has been completely transcended; an experience of supreme bliss when nothing of self remains. But Buddhism stresses that this does not mean annihilation. How can we understand this paradox? The *pneuma* concept provides one way of understanding it. *Pneuma* signifies that capacity for transcending oneself, of going out of oneself and beyond oneself, of losing oneself in communion with Reality: The more a person goes beyond himself, the more is the spiritual dimension of his life deepened, the more he becomes a true person. In transcending oneself one ceases to be a self-contained entity; but self-hood is always being fulfilled by being transcended. *Pneuma* signifies communion. The underlying principle is that communion differentiates by negating exclusive individuality and by perfecting personality. Personal identity will be retained in a complete harmony without that identity being expressed in the exclusiveness of self-contained individuality.

Anattā serves to stress the non-egocentric aspect and *Pneuma* the relational aspect of personhood. *Anattā-Pneuma* therefore signifies what might be called non-egocentric-relationality, or egoless mutuality. Thus, the *anattā-pneuma* formula captures in a nutshell, as it were, the essence of the nature of man.

10 The Spiritual Body

1. CORPORATE SOLIDARITY

(a) Personality and solidarity

Recent studies in biology, psychology, philosophy and biblical criticism are all agreed in rendering otiose the belief that man has within himself an immortal soul, distinct from the body, which survives death. According to these studies, there is nothing which can survive death. On the other hand the popular belief in the resurrection of the flesh, coming from Patristic times, and even included in the Apostle's Creed, has come to appear bizarre to contemplate. Between these two extremes is the biblical doctrine of the Resurrection of the Body. By Body (*sōma*) is here understood not the physical body but the 'Spiritual Body'.

The idea of the Spiritual Body (*sōma pneumatikon*), merged as it is with the doctrine of the Resurrection of the Body, which stands in sharp contrast to the doctrine of the immortality of the soul,[1] entered Christianity through the language of St Paul. The word body (*sōma*) is a key word in Paul's thought. He uses it in a variety of senses embracing the whole range of his thought.[2] But here we must necessarily confine ourselves to those aspects of the meaning of the term which have a bearing on our argument.

Basically *sōma* signifies the corporate solidarity of every individual as he is found in a personal-communal relationship. This is perfectly in line with the personal-communal nature of the self which we considered earlier. *Sōma* stands for both personality and solidarity in a mutual relationship. For St Paul, personality is bound up in the solidarity of historical existence; personal life has meaning and can be lived only in a social solidarity which is essentially a divinely ordained structure. This view of St Paul is rooted in the Hebrew understanding of man, although the word *sōma* has no immediate Old Testament background. Yet in its highest sense of corporate solidarity it has close affinities with the Hebrew word *bāsār*. This is very likely the point from which Paul started and developed his own theology.[3] We may summarise the meaning of the term *bāsār* in the words of J. A. T. Robinson as follows:

> *Bāsār* stands for the whole life-substance of men or beasts as organized in corporeal form. . . .
>
> True individuality was seen to be grounded solely in the indivisible responsibility of each man to God. . . . It rested, that is to say, in the uniqueness of the Divine Word or call to every man, which demanded from him an inalienable response. It did not in any way reside in him as *bāsār*. The flesh-body was not what partitioned a man off from his neighbour; it was rather what bound him in the bundle of life with all men and nature, so that he could never make his unique answer to God as an isolated individual, apart from his relation to his neighbour. The *bāsār* continued, even in the age of greater religious individualism, to represent the fact that personality is essentially social.[4]

Bāsār therefore signifies man's solidarity in finite existence and in social existence. As a finite being man is *bāsār*, is flesh-substance, which he shares with other men and beasts alike. As such, man shares the same fate as all finite beings. On the other hand, as a social being man stands in a responsible relationship to God and his neighbour. Man as *bāsār* is part of the finite world, and this world to which he is bound in the flesh is a fallen world, bearing, we may say, the marks of *anicca, dukkha* and *anattā*. But yet, this flesh-body is a God-given form of man's earthly existence. Thus man stands in an ambiguous relation to God and the world.

(b) Sarx and Sōma

St Paul preserves this ambiguity rather distinctly and sharply by using two Greek words, *sarx* and *sōma*, for the one Hebrew word *bāsār*.

Sarx like *bāsār* basically means the flesh-substance common to man and beast; it signifies the whole person in his external physical existence, in his weakness, sinfulness and mortality as a creature in contrast to God the creator; it means 'man in his "worldliness", in the solidarity of earthly existence'.[5] On the one hand *sarx* is a neutral term which signifies man's natural, historical and racial existence 'in the world': on the other hand it signifies the sinful state of existence in which man lives in the world. In the first case man lives in the flesh; in the latter case man lives 'after the flesh', although the

former phrase is often used in the sense of the latter. *Sarx* signifies
man's communal and natural (i.e. the material world) solidarity by
which he is involved in a divinely ordained structure of creation
which, at one and the same time, fulfils God's will and is
antagonistic to Him. Thus man in the flesh always stands in a
relation of ambiguity to God. Man 'in the flesh' has no hope. 'No
flesh should glory before God.'[6]

Sarx thus understood points to a doctrine of nihilism, but Paul
uses the other word *sōma* which negates a nihilistic view. While *sōma*
in its simplest non-ethical sense is synonymous with *sarx*, it differs
from *sarx* as it is the 'carrier' of men's resurrection. But there can be
no resurrection without a death of the whole person, of *sōma*. So we
see that St Paul identifies *sōma* with *sarx* – as the external man; as the
man 'in the flesh', as man apart from and in opposition to God; as
man doomed to nothingness. Hence, one may, with some re-
servations, agree with Oscar Cullman when he says,

> For Christian (and Jewish) thinking the death of the body is
> *also* destruction of God-created life. No distinction is made: even
> the life of our body is true life; death is the destruction of *all* life
> created by God. Therefore it is death and not the body which
> must be conquered by the Resurrection.[7]

But St Paul uses the term *sōma* in a distinctive sense. J. A. T.
Robinson distinguishes two strands in Paul's somatology:

> The *sōma*, or body, is the whole psycho-physical unity, made
> up of *sarx* and *psychē*, which constitutes man as distinguished from
> God. It is the nearest word in Greek for 'personality' for which
> none of the ancients had a term. But it is personality, as it were, *ad*
> *extra*. It is not the inner essence of what, theologically, makes man
> a person. This, for the Hebrew, is always something outside man
> himself – the call of God to a relationship of unique responsibility
> to Himself—and lies in the realm of spirit. It is personality as a
> phenomenon, the personality which the scientist investigates.
> And secondly, it is not personality as it has been defined
> abstractly in Western philosophical tradition, especially since
> Descartes. It is not the 'self', that which a man is in himself prior
> to and apart from all relationships into which he enters. *Sōma* is
> the whole man constituted as he is by the network of physical and
> mental relationships in which he is bound up with the continuum

of other persons and things. Though *sōma* definitely cannot be defined simply as man's 'body' (body as opposed to 'mind', is *sarx*, not *sōma*), it always means his personality seen as it were from outside rather than by introspection. It is his personality as materially and socially continuous with his environment.[8]

In the idea that man is called into a responsible relationship with God, *sōma* acquires a distinctive sense in opposition to *sarx*.

> . . . however much the two may come, through the Fall, to describe the same thing, in essence, *sarx* and *sōma* designate different aspects of the human relationship to God. While *sarx* stands for man, in his solidarity of creation, in his distance from God, *sōma* stands for man, in the solidarity of creation, as made for God.[9]

Thus, while there can be no resurrection of the flesh, there is a resurrection of the body. This does not mean, however, that *sarx* and *sōma* are two different and separable parts of man, one mortal and the other immortal. 'Each stands for the whole man differently regarded – man as wholly perishable, man as wholly destined for God.'[10] J. A. T. Robinson quotes an apt comment of P. Althaus:

> The body is, on the one hand, wholly *koilia*, that is, the sum of the sensual functions which make our earthly life possible; as such it passes away with this earthly world. On the other hand, the body is wholly *sōma*, that is, the career and object of our action, expression and form; as such it is a limb of the body of the risen Christ and will be raised with the personality (though the Hebrew would make no such distinction between the body and the personality). Because the one and the same body is both *koilia* and *sōma*, any concrete or objective expression of what dies, and what is preserved and purified through resurrection is impossible.[11]

From the above discussion of the meaning of the term *sōma* with its network of associations, there emerges one of the unparalleled ideas in which *sōma* is linked with Resurrection—it is the vehicle of the resurrection life. To this distinctive concept we now turn our attention.

2.   THE RESURRECTION BODY

(a) The re-created body

If we are to understand the Christian doctrine of the Resurrection aright, we must completely rid ourselves of the Greek idea that the material body is bad and evil, and so must be destroyed, and that the immortal soul survives death and cannot be destroyed. In Greek thought, the body was a tomb, as the phrase '*sōma sēma*' indicates, and the aim of life was to escape from this tomb. But for Paul, the aim of life was not escape from the body but the transformation of the body; a re-creation or resurrection of the whole person for life on a spiritual plane. This transformed body is the *sōma* imbued by the *pneuma*. *Sōma* is the basis of the resurrection life, but it rises to this new life not by any inherent power but by the power of the Spirit. Oscar Cullman puts this point sharply:

> Resurrection is a positive assertion: the whole man who has really died is recalled to life by a new act of creation by God. Something has happened – a miracle of creation! For something has also happened previously, something fearful: life formed by God has been destroyed.[12]

Thus we see that the Christian hope of survival rests solely on the doctrine of God and not on a doctrine of man's capacity. There is nothing in man, however noble, which is not subject to *anicca, dukkha* and *anattā* in the strictest sense of these words. Everything in man is finite, is *anicca* and must return to dust. 'Dust thou art and to dust thou shalt return.' There is nothing in man, no karmic force, that can endure beyond the grave – 'but the word of God endures for ever.' This 'word' is that by which God has called man into a relationship with Him and it is in this relationship that man finds his authentic being, and not in any condition of virtue or spirituality or merit or karmic force of his own. This view therefore reaches the utmost depths of the doctrine of *anattā*.

It may be noted at this point, that this view of the *body*, particularly in its Hebraic form, is in conformity with the *psycho-somatic* view of the self in modern scientific thinking to which Buddhism also claims some conformity. According to scientific opinion, a person is not a component of separable parts, nor is he in himself a separable unit of complete individuality, but has his place in a continuous stream (*santati* — flux or continuity) of plasm passing from one generation to another. There is no human individuality without sociality. The individual is continuous with the environment and is subject to change.[13] But Christianity differs in stressing that, while man participates in a corporate totality, individualisation cannot be eliminated.

(b) The principle of individualisation

The Christian doctrine of the Resurrection of the *body* is an assertion of the eternal significance and of the uniqueness of the individual person. As Reinhold Niebuhr puts it, the doctrine of the resurrection of the body 'implies that eternity will fulfil and not annul the riches and variety which the temporal process has elaborated', or, in other words, that 'eternal significance belongs to the whole unity of an historical realization in so far as it has brought all particularities into a harmony of the whole.'[14] Quoting St Paul, Niebuhr says that Paul

> . . . was convinced that 'flesh and blood cannot inherit the kingdom of God, neither doth corruption put on incorruption'. But this conviction did not drive him to the conclusion that everlasting life annuls all historical reality for which 'the body' is the symbol. He believed rather that 'it is sown a natural body and is raised a spiritual body', and that consummation means not to 'be unclothed, but clothed upon' (2 Cor. 5:4). In that succinct phrase the biblical hope of a consummation which will sublimate rather than annul the historical process is perfectly expressed.

The individuality of a person is expressed in every cell of his physical, mortal body. It manifests itself through the modes, features,[15] characteristics and expressions of the 'earthly body', making a person a self-identical individual persisting through the changes of life. The change that comes about at death is not from a life in a body to a life without a body or with a revivified material body, but from a life in one type of body (earthly body) to a life in another type of body (spiritual body). As F. J. Taylor has put it, the spiritual body

> . . . postulates an organ of personality, expressing and defining it and adapted to the conditions of a life in the eternal order, even

as the body of flesh and blood serves the same ends in the present order . . .[16]

This is what St Paul means when he says that there are terrestrial bodies such as those of birds and animals, and celestial bodies which have a 'glory' of their own.

The principle that the temporal has an eternal significance gives the physical body its real place in the religious life. It must not be despised and subjected to severe mortifications: it must not be disregarded and allowed to give way to licentiousness. This body can be the temple of the Holy Spirit. 'Do you not know that your body is a temple of the Holy Spirit within you which you have from God?'[17] It can participate in the mystical body of Christ: 'Do you not know that your bodies are members of Christ . . .?'[18] Christ can be manifested in our body, and we can glorify Him in our bodies.[19] Therefore, since the physical body is vitally, intimately and indissolubly connected with the spiritual body, we must keep it chaste and pure, and present our bodies 'as a living sacrifice, holy and acceptable to God, which is your spiritual worship'.[20]

3. THE SPIRITUAL BODY

(a) The link of continuity

The real truth behind the doctrine of the resurrection of the body is that the person continues as a person without the loss of identity. St Paul, using the analogy of the seed, says that it is put into the ground and that something different comes out of it, but this something different is what God has given according to his choice, 'to each kind of seed its own body.' St Paul is thus showing by way of analogy that at one and the same time there can be dissolution and difference and yet identity and continuity.[21] The earthly body will be buried and will disintegrate but 'it' will rise again in a different form. Yet the fact remains that it is the same person who rises, however different the resurrected body may be. As Emil Brunner puts it:

The concept of the spiritual body (*sōma pneumatikon*) expresses the wholeness of the person as an individuality created by God. I, this particular man, who am not to be confused with anyone else, I am to rise again. 'I have called thee by thy name; thou art mine' (Isaiah 43:1). That which is stamped upon us even in this earthly body, our individual character, is not to be annihilated but on the contrary to be perfected. 'It is not another self than mine that is created, but in "raising" me God preserves myself, in order to perfect it' (Althaus). The spiritual body is what is to belong to us in eternity as individual persons to whom God in eternity says 'Thou'.[22]

This earthly body is the organ of distinction, self-expression and individuality in one sphere of existence. The spiritual body is the organ of distinction, self-expression and individuality in another sphere and perfects the distinction, self-expression and individuality that belonged to the physical body. The individual will not be obliterated into nothingness or absorbed in the divine at death. He will continue to be the same individual preserving his identity in a different mode.

The phrase 'spiritual body' must not be confused with any spiritualistic or naturalistic notions. It must be understood as a double negation which negates both these wrong notions. On the one hand it negates the spiritualistic notion that the spiritual body is the transformation of this present physical body which survives death, or which is in a mysterious way revived at the Parousia. It also negates any dualistic notion of a spiritual entity that continues after death. Further it contradicts the theory of a continuing element such as *Viññāṇa, citta*, or karmic energy. On the other hand it negates the materialistic notion that flesh and blood can inherit the Kingdom of God.[23] Spirit is not a department of human biology or psychology. Spirit is, as Tillich says,

> God is present to man's spirit, invading it, transforming and elevating it beyond itself. A spiritual body then is a body which expresses the spiritually transformed total personality of man.[24]

Spirit is the principle of individualisation because it signifies a relationship with God into which man is called, and in which man becomes what he is because God, who is the God of Abraham, of Isaac, and of Jacob, calls each one by his own name to a unique fellowship with Him.

(b) Distinction and identity
Such an understanding of the meaning of 'spiritual body' gives new meaning to the well-known Buddhist phrase *na ca so na ca añño*. The

spiritual body which transcends conditioned existence is not the same as the body that lived (*na ca so*) because there is nothing 'taken up' from this body in the resurrection. The whole body dies. On the other hand the spiritual body has an identity and continuity with the physical body, it is no other (*na ca añño*) because *sōma* is, as Althaus, quoted earlier, put it: 'the career and object of our action, expression and form.' But this identity is what is given in a relationship apart from which no individual exists, and it is in this relationship that the individual continues to live here and in the hereafter.

4.   THE 'REPLICA' THEORY

We said that the spiritual body is the organ of distinction, self-expression, and individuality. These are relational terms. There can be distinction only in a relation. The distinction between X and Y can be seen only in a relation between the two. Self-expression is possible only through interaction and individuality through growth in mutuality. The physical body is the organ which holds these three together in this earthly sphere of existence. At death this body is completely destroyed. In the resurrection God re-creates anew a 'body' suited to a new sphere of existence in which distinction, self-expression and individuality are preserved. Because this is a re-creation the spiritual body is not the same as the self which existed in an earthly body (*na ca so*). But because the re-created body preserves the distinction, self-expression and individuality which belonged to the earthly body, the re-created body is not a different person (*na ca añño*).

Thus the truth of *anattā* requires the doctrine of resurrection or re-creation. If *anattā* is real there cannot be natural survival. To affirm the continuity of one's own karmic force or memory, contradicts the truth of *anattā*. Nothing in man can survive death. This is the truth of *anattā* and *anicca*. Survival is possible only if God re-creates a new being. This is the truth of resurrection. For the Christian the primary ground for the hope of the hereafter is solely his relationship of faith and trust in God.

Some modern theologians who reject the view that man's soul persists after the decease of the body have sought to account for the post-mortem identity in God's memory of us.[25] After I die I will cease to exist but God will go on remembering me, and to be remembered by God is to have my identity preserved. In other words I participate in eternity by being remembered by God.

John Hick has critically examined this view in *Death and Eternal Life*[26] and found it wanting. According to him this view postulates 'a static, frozen immortality'.[27] He advocates a much more helpful view, that at the moment of our death God creates 'an exact psycho-physical "replica" of the deceased person'.[28] He is using the word 'replica' not in the sense of a duplicate but in a special sense (please note quotes) to give content to the notion of resurrection. He speaks of resurrection as 'replication'. Using an illustration he explains what he means:

> The pattern of the body can be regarded as a message that is in principle capable of being coded, transmitted, and then translated back into its original form, as sight and sound patterns may be transmitted by radio and translated back into sound and picture.[29]

We should be quite clear that it is not the living organism, the body itself but 'its encoded form that is transmitted'.[30] This encoded form will, as Norbert Wiener, whom Hick quotes, says, contain

> the whole pattern of the human body, of the human brain with its memories and cross-connections, so that a hypothetical receiving instrument could re-embody these messages in appropriate matter, capable of continuing the processes already in the body and the mind, and of maintaining the integrity needed for this continuation by a process of homeostasis.[31]

So it is possible to speak of the resurrection or 'replication' of the person who dies as the same one who was 'encoded' in his earthly life.

We might say that this encoded form contains the whole of man's *karma* – his thoughts, words and deeds. But here we use *karma* in a special sense. It has no inherent power to transmit or re-embody itself. It has to be brought to life by an act of creation.

This re-created 'replica' theory emphasises three important points. Firstly, just as the replica is not the result of self-generation, so life after death is not self-generated. Secondly, just as a replica is not the same as the original, so the one who is resurrected is not exactly the same as the one before death (*na ca so*). Thirdly, because replication is a re-creation from the encoded form of the psycho-physical organism, the 'replica' is not anything other than the original (*na ca añño*). This replica theory thus gives us a new understanding of the truth implied in the formula *na ca so, na ca añño*.

11 Progressive Sanctification

1. THE DOUBLE PREDESTINATION THEORY

We have seen the difficulties which the theory of Karma and rebirth presents. The notion that at death a person passes to everlasting damnation in Hell or eternal happiness in Heaven, considered to be the orthodox Christian view, presents even greater difficulties. This is referred to as the 'Double Predestination' theory and is popularly known as the theory of 'One life on earth followed by Heaven or Hell for Eternity.' Many have found this theory theologically unsound and far less comforting than the theory of Karma and rebirth.

Francis Bowen, criticising this theory, says:

Our life on earth is rightly held to be a discipline and a preparation for a higher and eternal life hereafter, but if limited to the duration of a single mortal body, it is so brief as to seem hardly sufficient for so grand a purpose. Three score years and ten must surely be an inadequate preparation for eternity.[1]

Christian theologians have rejected this notion in no uncertain terms. Nicholas Berdyaev calls it 'a devilish notion of eternal punishment'.[2] He further says:

There is something hideous and morally revolting in the idea of eternal torments as just retribution for the crimes and sins of a short moment of life. Eternal damnation as the result of things done in a short period of time is one of the most disgusting of human nightmares. The doctrine of reincarnation, which has obvious advantages, involves, however, another nightmare: the nightmare of endless incarnation, of infinite wanderings along dark passages; it finds the solution of man's destiny in the cosmos and not in God. . . . The idea of hell is particularly revolting when it is interpreted in a legalistic sense. Such an interpretation is common and vulgar and must be completely banished from religious ethics, philosophy and theology.[3]

Paul Tillich says:

> One cannot make the moment of death decisive for man's ultimate destiny. In the case of infants, children and under-developed adults, for example, this would be a complete absurdity. In the case of mature people it disregards innumerable elements which enter every mature personal life and cause profound ambiguity.[4]

The late Archbishop William Temple asks: 'Are there not, however, many passages which speak of the endless torment of the lost?' and he himself answers: 'No; as far as my knowledge goes there is none at all.'[5] There is no one bad enough to go straight into eternal damnation and conversely there is no one good enough to go straight to eternal bliss. The wrong notion regarding the once-and-for-all decisiveness of the moment of death and endless torment is mainly due to literalistic distortions of such symbols as 'the unquenchable fire', 'the worm that dieth not', and the mixing up of such terms as *Hades, Hell, Sheol, Gehenna, Paradise, Abraham's bosom* and *Heaven*, which are relics of an archaic cosmology. The sense in which these symbols and terms are used must be discerned by a careful linguistic analysis which is not possible here. All that is possible is to indicate the results of modern biblical scholarship.

In an article on 'The Future Life in Contemporary Theology', William Strawson indicates the direction in which modern biblical scholarship is moving:

> The old rigid distinction between the saved and the lost is giving way to a view which is much less dogmatic and, many will think, much more Christian. Instead of attempting to divide man into two categories, we should think of the process of divine activity in which the positive elements are developed and the negative diminished. This process Tillich describes as 'essentialisation' – eternal life is the development of the positive elements in life, and because of the ambiguity of life, often there is little positive to be developed. But no man is totally evil, any more than anyone is totally good; the idea of a two-fold destiny contradicts the self-manifestation of God and the nature of man.

Double pre-destination is only the extreme ('demonic') form of this separation, which Tillich thinks is wrong because it makes destiny too much an individual affair, and at the same time disregards the ambiguities of human existence. If anyone raises the alarm and sees in this a resurgence of 'universalism', even Karl Barth can be brought in to support a new appraisal of this less rigid and more open view of human prospects (see his 'The Humanity of God'). Brunner also denies the idea of the saved /lost distinction, but tries to retain the notion of judgement, by saying that the word of condemnation is to be regarded as aimed at salvation, which is always the ultimate purpose of God.[6]

Here we have a concept of progress and development, of progressive sanctification, through which the self continues to grow after the termination of the physical body in this life. There is a 'period of waiting' until the final consummation, during which time there will be a progressive actualisation of the positive and a diminishing of the negative, until all things are perfected in the Kingdom of God.

2. PROGRESSIVE SANCTIFICATION

For more than one reason we need to accept some such state of 'progressive sanctification after death'. For one thing we need it for a Christian theodicy – defence of the goodness of God in the face of suffering and evil in His world. If, according to the double pre-destination theory, we are at the moment of death transmuted in the twinkling of an eye into perfect beings or condemned for eternal damnation, then, as John Hick says, 'the whole earthly travail of faith and moral effort is rendered needless'.[7] John Hick, having convincingly argued that suffering and evil in God's world are not without moral purpose, the recognition of which is essential for a theodicy, says:

If, then, we assume that such sufferings are not eternal and hence morally pointless, but rather temporal and redemptive in purpose, we are led to postulate an existence or existences beyond the grave in which the moral structure of reality is borne in upon the individual, and in which his self-centredness is gradually broken through by a 'godly sorrow' (2 Cor: 7:10) that represents the inbreaking of reality. Such an idea is, of course, not far from the traditional Roman Catholic notion of purgatorial experiences occurring (for those who are in a state of grace) between death and entry into the final heavenly Kingdom in which God shall be all in all. Because of the grave abuses that helped to provoke the Reformation of the sixteenth century the word 'purgatory' has a bad sound in many ears; and some of the Protestant theologians who have entertained an essentially similar idea have preferred to use instead the term 'progressive sanctification after death'. The thought behind this phrase is that as sanctification (or perfecting) in this life comes partly through suffering, the same is presumably true of the intermediate state in which the sanctifying process, begun on earth, continues towards its completion, its extent and duration being determined by the degree of unsanctification remaining to be overcome at the time of death.[8]

The bloodcurdling imagery, the innumerable superstitions, and the corrupt practices connected with the doctrine of Purgatory have made it most repugnant and abhorrent to Protestants, but Protestant theologians are finding some such conception indispensable for a reasonable understanding of Christian eschatology. For example, John Macquarrie makes a strong case for the acceptance of such a doctrine:

If . . . we think of heaven and hell as limits to be approached rather than final conditions in which to remain; if we try to visualize eschatology in dynamic rather than static terms; if we refuse to draw any hard and fast line between the 'righteous' and the 'wicked', or between the 'elect' and the 'reprobate'; if we reject the idea that God's reconciling work is restricted to people living at this particular moment and believe that His reconciliation can reach anywhere so that it makes sense to pray for the departed; above all, if we entertain any universalist hopes of salvation for the whole creation, then we are committed to the belief in an intermediate state, whether or not we call it 'purgatory' . . . Heaven, purgatory, and hell are not sharply separated, but form a kind of continuum through which the soul may move, perhaps from near-annihilation of sin to closest union with God. . . . This whole movement is a process of purification.[9]

We need to purge the doctrine of Purgatory of its traditional imagery and restate the truth underlying it. Basically, purgatory symbolises the process of purging the distorting elements in a person; it is a process of cleansing by which a person is fitted for his ultimate destiny. The kind of 'suffering' envisaged in purgatory must not be understood as 'mere suffering' as a penalty for wrongs done, but as a painful surrender of the ego-centred self, the losing of self, the discovery that one is *anattā* in the process of finding one's true being. Purgatory is a process of spiritual death and rebirth, of progressive sanctification, a process which begins in this very life. In the words of Romano Guardini, 'death upon death has to be endured so that the new life may arise.'[10]

Here we have a concept of progress and development in which the mental and spiritual qualities of a person continue to grow after death. In other words there is an 'intermediate state' from now till the final consummation, during which there is a progressive actualisation of the positive and a diminishing of the negative.[11] This conception of an 'intermediate state' is not an imaginary creation to overcome a theological problem; it has a basis in the scriptures.

3. THE BIBLICAL BASIS

The locus classicus of this concept of the 'intermediate state', according to C. Harris, is the parable of Dives and Lazarus.[12] Dives the rich man died and he went to 'Hades', a word which means the abode of the departed spirits. The fact that Jesus also descended into 'Hades' to preach to the departed spirits there, shows that 'Hades' was not a place of ultimate doom. Lazarus the beggar died, and he was carried by the angels to 'Abraham's bosom', 'a common rabbinical designation of the intermediate abode of bliss.'[13] It was a common figure used by the Jews to indicate paternal tenderness (Abraham being the father of the Jews),[14] love and happiness, as contrasted with the torments of Hades. The phrase was widely used in early Christian writings as a synonym for the intermediate state.[15] From this there emerge two lines of thought: that, in the intermediate period between now and the Consummation there is (*a*) 'a state of painful confinement in which the unrighteous expiated their crimes, and were in some cases cleansed from sin', and (*b*) 'a state of blissful expectancy in which the righteous awaited their reward.'[16] In both states there is a period of waiting, of purgation and progressive sanctification.

There are a number of passages in support of the first line of thought, from which presumably has been deduced the article of faith found in the Apostles' Creed, that Christ descended into Hades. Two passages often quoted in this connection are from the First Epistle of St Peter.[17]

The first is 1 Peter 3:18–20. In this the idea of Christ's preaching to the dead is particularised:

> Christ also died for sins once for all, the righteous for the unrighteous, that He might bring us to God, being put to death in the flesh but made alive in the spirit, in which He went and preached to the spirits in prison, who formerly did not obey, when God's patience waited in the days of Noah, during the building of the Ark.[18]

The second is 1 Peter 4:6. In this the idea of Christ preaching to the dead is generalised:

> For this is why the gospel was preached even to the dead, that though judged in the flesh like men, they might live in the spirit like God.[19]

In a number of passages this idea is universalised. We shall look at a few of them.

In St John 5:25 we read:

> Truly, truly, I say to you, the hour is coming, and now is, when the dead will hear the voice of the Son of God, and those who hear will live.

The 'dead' may here mean the spiritually dead.

In Philippians 2:9—11 the ultimate triumph of Jesus in every part of the universe is stated:

> Therefore God has highly exalted Him, and bestowed on Him the name which is above every name, that at the name of Jesus every knee should bow, in heaven and on earth and under the earth, and every tongue confess that Jesus Christ is Lord, to the glory of God the Father.[20]

In Revelation 5:13 there is a similar passage:

> And I heard every creature in heaven and on earth and under the earth, and in the sea, and all therein, saying: 'To him who sits upon the throne and to the Lamb be blessing and honour and glory and might for ever and ever'.[21]

From all this emerges one great truth which William Barclay expresses, with particular reference to the two passages in 1 Peter, as follows:

> If Christ descended into Hades, and preached there, then there is no corner of the universe into which the message of grace has not come. There is in this passage the solution of one of the most haunting questions raised by the Christian faith: What is to happen to those who lived before Jesus Christ, and to those to whom the gospel never came? There can be no salvation without repentance, and how can repentance come to those who have never been confronted with the love and holiness of God? If there is no other name by which man may be saved, what is to happen to those who never heard that name? This is the point that Justin Martyr fastened on long ago: 'The Lord, the Holy God of Israel, remembered His dead, those sleeping in the earth, and came down to them to tell them the good news of salvation.' The doctrine of the descent into Hades conserves the precious truth that no man who ever lived is left without a sight of Christ, and without the offer of the salvation of God.[22]

To those who have never really had a chance in this life, either because they were born blind or with other physical defects which have marred their lives, or because they have met with misfortune or obstacles in an evil society which shut the doors to progress, the doctrine of the descent into Hades provides not only comfort but a satisfactory answer to the question: What justice is there if the iniquities in this life cannot be compensated?

To those who have been rebellious, who have sinned against the truth, who have turned away from the light, the intermediate state involves anguish and remorse, a torturing unrest in the knowledge of having fallen short of the goal about which one becomes acutely conscious when the earthly limitations are removed at death. The degree of anguish and torture corresponds to the degree of the separation from Reality. The story of Dives and Lazarus illustrates this distance and anguish, which are symbolised by the term Hell (*Gehenna*).[23] Hell is not a place situated in the underworld. It is not an ontological reality but a psychological experience which a person can have in this life as well as in the next.[24]

The second line of thought relates to the 'righteous', to those who have responded to Reality or, in Christian terms, those who believe in Christ; for the Christian believes that the ultimate Reality was manifest in Christ. It may be that there are people who have responded to that Reality which Christians call God without using this term God or even while rejecting it. We could therefore agree with Jacques Maritain when he says: 'Under many names, names which are not that of God, in ways only known to God, the interior act of the soul's thought can be directed towards a reality which in fact truly may be God.'[25] This same idea is expressed in the following statement taken from a document of the World Council of Churches:

> Now and hereafter Christ brings grace and judgement to all men. God has no favourites, but in every nation the man who is god-fearing and does what is right is acceptable to Him (Acts 10:34—35, cf. Rom: 2:6—16). We draw attention to the formulation of this truth in the Vatican Council's Dogmatic Constitution on the Church: 'Those also can attain to everlasting salvation who through no fault of their own do not know the gospel of Christ or His Church, yet sincerely seek God and, moved by grace, strive by their deeds to do His will as it is known to them through the dictates of conscience.'[26]

This response to Reality, this relationship to God is what the Bible calls 'Eternal life'. God alone is Eternal. Man is mortal. But man can become eternal by coming into a relationship with the Eternal. Since man is not in himself immortal, since he has no immortal soul, Eternal life is not a human achievement, although man has his part to play. Eternal life is that which comes from God and which man appreciates by responding to the Eternal (the *Amata*); it is life in the Spirit.

This response is a response of faith: 'God so loved the world that He gave His only Son, that whoever believes in Him should not perish but have eternal life.'[27] It involves knowledge. 'This is eternal life, that they know Thee the only true God, and Jesus Christ whom

Thou hast sent.'[28] Knowledge here means intimate relationship. Eternal life originates in the love of God; its possession and achievement depend on the response of faith leading to an intimate relationship with God.

The concept of eternal life in the New Testament does not simply mean a life that goes on for ever and ever. The essential emphasis about eternal life is on quality rather than on duration. Love is the quality of eternal life, for 'God is Love'; and love is a relationship. This relationship, the essence of which is love, is a relationship which begins here and now and continues in the hereafter. It is in and through love that resurrection or 'replication' takes place. The 'encoded' form of the person takes place in God's love. This love is, we could say, the 'receiving instrument' (to borrow the term Norbert Wiener uses[29]) on which the encoding takes place.

This idea of eternal life thus means that the life to come is a continuation of the life in this world in its encoded form. The corporate solidarity which begins here does not end at death. The personal-communal context of life in which alone a 'person' exists through replication as an authentic self, continues in the intermediate state. This means that there is growth and development through individualisation and participation, even in the life to come. At death man is not automatically transformed into a perfect being. He must grow into perfection. He must be transformed or progressively sanctified from one degree of glory to another.[30] Progressive sanctification in terms of *anattā-pneuma* means the progressive realisation of anattā-ness or egolessness by the elimination of the negative elements in man, and the progressive actualisation of pneuma-ness by the development of the positive elements until individualisation and participation reach perfection in the Kingdom of God, through a process of continuous recreation.

As early as the fourth century A.D. Gregory of Nyssa gave expression to this idea of progressive sanctification as follows:

Thus though the new grace we may obtain is greater than what we had before, it does not put a limit on our final goal; rather, for those who are rising in perfection, the limit of the good that is attained becomes the beginning of the discovery of higher goods. Thus they never stop rising, moving from one new beginning to the next, and the beginning of ever greater graces is never limited of itself. For the desire of those who thus rise never rests in what

they can already understand; but by an ever greater and greater
desire, the soul keeps rising constantly to another which lies
ahead, and thus it makes its way through ever higher regions
towards the Transcendent.[31]

From very early times one famous verse has been pressed into the
service of this idea of the stages of development. This verse is St John
14:2: 'In my Father's house are many mansions', as the Authorized
Version has it. The important word here is 'mansions' (Greek *monai*)
which the Revised Standard Version translates as 'rooms'; the New
English Bible as 'dwelling-places'; Moffatt as 'abodes'; and Wey-
mouth as 'resting places'. One possible interpretation is that in the
'Father's house' there is room for all; abiding places in which to stay
on. Some commentators consider this the only possible meaning
because the only other place in the New Testament where this word
is used is in verse 23 of the same chapter, where it can only mean
'abode' or 'home' in the sense of a permanent habitation.

Another interpretation that has fascinated people down the ages is
that this word *monai* means resting-places where pilgrims on their
way to eternity stop for training and instruction, as they proceed
further and further towards the final goal. The Greek writer
Pausanias supports the interpretation of the word *monai* as meaning
'stages on the way'. Origen and Clement of Alexandria also held
this view. William Temple's interpretation of *monai* also supports
such a view. 'The resting places (monai)', he says, 'are wayside
caravanserais-shelters at stages along the road where travellers may
rest on their journey. . . . It may be that we are still far from perfect
fellowship with the Father. . . . We have a long journey of many
days before us ere our pilgrimage is accomplished. But there are, by
God's mercy, *many resting-places.*' Continuing, Temple says, 'These
many resting-places, marking the stages of our spiritual growth, are in
the *Father*'s house. If we are travelling heavenwards, we are already
in heaven.'[32] Progressive sanctification begins here and now and
continues stage by stage in the hereafter, till our fellowship with God
is perfect.

12 The Kingdom of God – Community of Love

1. NIBBĀNA: EXPERIENCE OF SELF-NEGATION

The concept of the Kingdom of God has, because of certain ecclesiastical and sacramental developments of Christianity, the social gospel movement and some forms of religious socialism, lost its relevance for modern man. Its reinstatement as a 'living symbol', as Tillich points out, 'may come from the encounter of Christianity with Asiatic religions, especially Buddhism', and particularly in relation to the concept of *Nibbāna*.[1] A reinterpretation of the meaning of the kingdom of God in relation to *Nibbāna* could very well be the task for a book by itself. All that is attempted in this chapter is to indicate certain directions along which we could move towards a mutual understanding of these two concepts, bearing in mind the problem we are dealing with.

Whatever *Nibbāna* means, at least it means two things: the extinction of desire (which includes all defilements) and the experience of well-being, the latter being an outcome of the former. In general Buddhists emphasise the fact that *Nibbāna* is an experience and that it is only those who have that experience who can know what *Nibbāna* is. Self-negation is an essential aspect of this experience. This does not mean annihilation of the self but an experience in which the notion of 'I', 'me' and 'mine', of separate individuality, disappears. Since 'self' is at the heart of man's problem, the 'self' must be conquered if the goal is to be realised. The egocentric life of craving and self-interest must be put to an end by the deliberate denying of the self. On this, up to a point, Christianity can agree with Buddhism. There is support for this in the scriptures as well as in the experience of Christians. The well-known words of Jesus come immediately to our mind:

If any man would come after me, let him deny himself and take up his cross and follow me. For whoever would save his life will lose it, and whoever loses his life for my sake will find it.[2]

What does it mean to deny oneself? William Barclay comments on the above verse as follows:

> To deny oneself is to say 'I do not know myself.' It is to ignore the very existence of oneself. It is to treat the self as if it did not exist. Usually we treat ourselves as if our self was far and away the most important thing in the world. If we are to follow Jesus we must obliterate self and forget that self exists.[3]

What does obliteration of the self, forgetting that self exists, really mean in experience? This has been expressed by some in language that has a Buddhist flavour.

To Meister Eckhart, a saint and mystic of the thirteenth century, it meant the complete absence of desire, even the desire to do the will of God:

> Supposing someone asks me, what then is the poor man who wills nothing? I should answer this: As long as it can be said of a man that it is in his will to do the will of God, that man has not the poverty I am speaking of, because he has the will to satisfy the will of God, which is not as it should be. If he is genuinely poor, a man is free from his created will as he was when he was not. I tell you by the eternal truth, as long as you possess the will to do the will of God, and have the least desire for eternity and for God, you are not really poor. The poor man wills nothing, knows nothing, wants nothing.[4]

To Isaac Pennington, a Puritan and Quaker, it meant considering himself a 'nobody'. 'I am a worm, I am poor, I am nothing, less than nothing as in myself,' he said.

To the writer of the Theologia Germanica (an anonymous mystical writing of the fourteenth century) self-denial in the first instance meant the perception of the nothingness of separate creaturely life:

> Man of himself and his own is nothing, has nothing, can do and is capable of nothing, but only infirmity, evil and wickedness. No

one shall dare to take goodness to himself, for that belongs to God and his Goodness only.[5]

To Henry Suso the German mystic, it meant the entire and complete renunciation of the notion of selfhood:

'Lord, tell me', says the Servitor, 'What remains to a blessed soul which has wholly renounced itself?'

Truth says, 'When the good and faithful servant enters into the joy of his Lord, he is inebriated by the riches of the house of God; for he feels, in an ineffable degree, that which is felt by an inebriated man. He forgets himself, he is no longer conscious of his selfhood; he disappears and loses himself in God, and becomes one spirit with Him, as a drop of water which is drowned in a great quantity of wine. For even as such a drop disappears, taking the colour and taste of wine, so it is with those who are in full possession of blessedness. All human desires are taken from them in an indescribable manner, they are wrapt from themselves, and are immersed in the Divine Will. If it were otherwise, if there remained in the man some human thing that was not absorbed, those words of Scripture which say that God must be all in all would be false. His being remains, but in another form, in another glory, and in another power. And all this is the result of entire and complete renunciation.[6]

Thus in the Christian mystical tradition, there is something strikingly analogous to the Buddhist notion of the need to strip oneself of the notion of I, Me, Mine. Summarising this central feature of Christian mysticism, Evelyn Underhill says:

All the mystics agree that the stripping off of personal initiative, the I, the Me, the Mine, utter renouncement, or 'self-naughting' – self-abandonment to the direction of a larger Will – is an imperative condition of the attainment of the unitive life. The temporary denudation of the mind, whereby the contemplative made space for the vision of God, must now be applied to the whole life. Here, they say, there is a final swallowing up of that wilful I-hood which we ordinarily recognize as ourselves. It goes for ever, and something new is established in its room. The self is made part of the mystical Body of God; and, humbly taking its place in the corporate life of Reality, would 'fain be to the Eternal Goodness what his own hand is to a man'.[7]

To explain this mystical relationship to God, Jakob Boehme uses a striking illustration:

> I give you an earthly similitude of this. Behold a bright flaming piece of iron, which of itself is dark and black, and the fire so penetrateth and shineth through the iron, that it giveth light. Now, the iron doth not cease to be; it is iron still: and the source (or property) of the fire retaineth its own propriety: it doth not take the iron into it, but it penetrateth (and shineth) through the iron; and it is iron then as well as before, free in itself: and so also is the source or property of the fire. In such a manner is the soul set in the Deity; the Deity penetrateth through the soul, and dwelleth in the soul, yet the soul doth not comprehend the Deity, but the Deity comprehendeth the soul, but doth not alter it (from being a soul) but only giveth it the divine source (or property) of the Majesty.[8]

Evelyn Underhill gives three characteristics of the highest reaches of the contemplative life, as follows:

> The chief, in fact the one essential, preliminary is that pure surrender of selfhood, or 'self-naughting', which the trials of the Dark Night tended to produce. Only the thoroughly detached, 'naughted soul' is 'free', says the *Mirror of Simple Souls*, and the Unitive State is essentially a state of free and filial participation in Eternal Life. The chief marks of the state itself are (1) a complete absorption in the interests of the Infinite, under whatever mode It happens to be apprehended by the self; (2) a consciousness of sharing Its strength, acting by Its authority, which results in a complete sense of freedom, an invulnerable serenity, and usually urges the self to some form of heroic effort or creative activity; (3) the establishment of the self as a 'power for life', a centre of energy, an actual parent of spiritual vitality in other men.[9]

On this level of experience Christianity has come very close to the Buddhist understanding of selflessness. But unlike Buddhism, Christianity says that it is only by abandoning oneself to God that one can die to self. The self cannot be denied by directly aiming at the self. In trying to negate self by such negative and introverted ascetic practices one only succeeds in intensifying and affirming the self. It is a psychological fact that conscious self-denial makes a man self-possessed and self-absorbed. So the sovereign cure for the problem of self, as Christianity sees it, is to turn one's attention away from self to God and allow the divine reality to occupy the centre of one's being. The Theologia Germanica has a passage which illuminates this truth:

> A man should understand and be so free from himself, that is, from self-hood, I-hood, me, mine, and the like, that in all things he should no more seek and regard himself and his own, than if he did not exist, and should take as little account of himself as if he were not, and another has done all his works. Likewise, he should count all creatures for nothing. What is there, then, which is and which we may count for somewhat? Answer: Nothing but that which we call God.[10]

The experience of self-negation is a state of being immutable, indifferent and insensible to self when nothing is left but Divine Reality. In this I – Thou relationship one loses oneself completely, and in losing oneself one finds oneself. Exclusive individuality is negated, but personality finds fulfilment. This state is partially experienced in this life in all levels of being, but it reaches its ultimate state in the Kingdom of God, when, to use Tillich's words, 'Individualization reaches its perfect form which we call a "person" and participation reaches its perfect form which we call "communion".'

2. THE KINGDOM: UNION AND DIFFERENTIATION

The all-embracing and crowning idea in the New Testament is that of the Kingdom of God, or in other words the Community of Love, for 'Kingdom' implies a Community, and God is Love. This Kingdom or Community embraces all dimensions of being – the individual and the social, the historical and the trans-historical. This agrees with the multidimensional unity of life and the personal-communal nature of being which we considered earlier. Thus the Kingdom of God has a double quality embracing the particular and the universal in such a way that the individual is transcended in a social reality and the historical in a trans-historical reality without any aspect being denied, but rather fulfilled. That which upholds the double quality is love, which is the supreme manifestation of Spirit.

In the New Testament the concept of the Kingdom signifies the kingly rule, the rule of God, His sovereignty. It is intended to affirm that God reigns in all aspects of personal, social and historical life in order to perfect all things and bring all things to a final fulfilment. The idea that all things move towards a consummation introduces an eschatological element, so that we live in hope, in the expectation of the fulfilment towards which history runs. The Kingdom of God therefore symbolises the completion, fulfilment and the final meaning of life and history. Yet it is something which God gives, not something which men achieve; it is God's Kingdom, God's work, not a Utopia or a new social order which man creates for himself.

In the idea of the Kingdom of God, I suggest, we have an answer to the Buddhist quest for self-negation as well as for a form of self-fulfilment, without one contradicting the other. The Kingdom of God is a perfect union of the universal and the particular; it is the actualisation of universal love in which the element of individualisation is not eliminated in union and participation. There can be no union without participation in union. That means that perfect union implies a differentiation of individual centres of participation. The underlying principle is that union differentiates by negating exclusive individuality and perfecting personality.

We must be careful not to confuse individuality with personality. Pierre Teilhard de Chardin writes with remarkable insight on this question:

> In trying to separate itself as much as possible from others, the element individualises itself, but in doing so it becomes retrograde and seeks to drag the world backwards towards plurality and into matter. In fact it diminishes itself and loses itself. To be ourselves is in the opposite direction, in the direction of convergence with all the rest, that we must advance towards the 'other'. The goal of ourselves, the acme of our originality, is not our individuality but our person; and, according to the evolutionary structure of the world, we can only find our person by uniting together. There is no mind without synthesis. The same law holds good from top to bottom. The true ego grows in inverse

proportion to 'egotism'. Like the Omega which attracts it, the element becomes personal when it universalizes itself.[11]

One becomes a person not by separation but by participation. By separation the individual 'materialises' himself; by participation the individual 'spiritualises' himself. The former is a retrograde step that tends towards annihilation; the latter is a progressive step that leads to the life in the Kingdom in which union is perfected.

Perfect union implies two things:

(*a*) On the one hand there can be no perfect union without the complete loss of self. As long as a person has an exclusive notion of 'I', 'me' or 'mine' he cannot participate in a fellowship and he thus excludes himself. In trying to separate oneself from the others and sever all person-to-person connections a person 'individualises' himself, as Pierre Teilhard says, and in so doing he loses his real nature by becoming 'materialised', which ultimately could lead to the extinction of the self. The Arahat ideal in Buddhism appears to move in this direction of 'individualising', and if it is so, *Nirvāna* as the complete extinction of the self would appear to be the logical conclusion. When Jesus said, 'He that seeketh himself shall lose himself', He probably meant the possibility of the extinction of the self which 'individualises' itself and separates itself from fellowship with others.

The right direction is not separation but integration. But for a perfect integration there must be a total surrender of the self, a complete losing of oneself in communion. The notion of self must completely disappear. In this way, exclusive individuality will be completely negated. Self-contained, self-regarding individuality must completely disappear before a perfect union becomes possible. Thus, perfect union or communion can be said to mean the complete 'extinction' of self, i.e. the dying out of separate individuality. We could thus speak of this goal in the negative sense in which the term *Nirvāna* is used. *Taṇhā* (craving) and the exclusive notion of 'I', 'me', 'mine', which is the basis of *taṇhā*, is conquered. To the question: 'Who is it that enters there?' we could give the traditional Buddhist answer, 'No one', for there is no individualised, self-existent being that enters there; there is no immortal soul that inherits the Kingdom. In this sense *Nirvāna* could be taken as an aspect of the Kingdom of God; it is a spiritual dimension within the Kingdom.

(*b*) On the other hand, perfect union implies a differentiation.

Pierre Teilhard explains this principle of differentiation as follows:

> In any domain – whether it be cells of a body, the members of a society or the elements of a spiritual synthesis – *union differentiates*. In every organised whole, the parts perfect themselves and fulfil themselves. Through neglect of this universal rule many a system of pantheism has led us astray to the cult of a great All in which individuals were supposed to be merged like a drop in the ocean or like a dissolving grain of salt. Applied to the case of the summation of consciousness, the law of union rids us of this perilous and recurrent illusion. No, following the confluent orbits of their centres, the grains of consciousness do not tend to lose their outlines and blend, but, on the contrary, to accentuate the depth and incommunicability of their *egos*. The more 'other' they become in conjunction, the more they find themselves as 'self'. How could it be otherwise since they are steeped in Omega? Could a centre dissolve? Or rather, would not its particular way of dissolving be to supercentralize itself?[12]

The more 'other', the more 'self'. 'Union differentiates.' But this differentiation is not a mark of exclusive individuality. It is an identity within a totality. It is union, not in the sense of absorption but in the sense of communion. It is an identity, not in the sense of a persisting self-contained entity, but in the sense of a 'recognisability' within a relationship. We become persons only in a relationship. I am known only in relation to the other and not in what I am by myself. I am recognised not as an individual in separation, but as a person in relationship. The basis of this relationship could be stated as follows: You are, therefore I am; I exist because you exist. I am more myself when I cease to be myself in the other. 'The more other, the more self' is a profound principle. By becoming more other, ultimately I become wholly other, when participation is perfected. I become one with the whole. This is the Hindu quest.[13] By becoming wholly other, one ceases wholly to be an individual. Self-contained, self-conscious individuality disappears. This is the Buddhist quest – the negation of self, self-abandonment, death to self. But because 'union differentiates', identity is preserved in a unity. This is neither absorption nor dissolution. Thus Christianity does not fall into either the error of eternalism or nihilism. In the final state, we shall cease completely to be separate individuals, as implied in the nirvanic principle of self-negation, but we shall be fully persons in keeping with the principle that union or communion differentiates.

3. SELF-LOSS AND SELF-GAIN THROUGH LOVE

It is love alone that is capable of uniting in such a way as to negate exclusive individuality and complete and fulfil personality.[14] On this point Pierre Teilhard again writes with remarkable insight:

> Love alone is capable of uniting living beings in such a way as to complete and fulfil them, for it alone takes them and joins them by what is deepest in themselves. This is a fact of daily experience. At what moment do lovers come into the most complete possession of themselves if not when they say they are lost in each other? In truth, does not love every instant achieve all around in the couple or in the team the magic feat, the fact reputed to be contradictory, of 'personalising' by totalising? And if that is what it can achieve daily on a small scale, why should it not repeat this one day in world-wide dimensions?[15]

'Personalising by totalising' – that signifies something of the meaning of the Kingdom of God. This is achieved by love which is the supreme manifestation of Spirit. The loss of exclusive individuality, which constitutes the fulfilment of personality, is the essence of the experience of love. The Kingdom of God or the Community of Love in this sense is participation in the individuality-negating, personality-fulfilling love.

Love is the supreme manifestation of Spirit. That which links together persons in community is love. Love is the affinity of being with being; it is the urge towards the union of the separated. One cannot be in love and not be in relation.

Love has a two-fold character; it is self-sacrificing and self-regarding; centrifugal and centripetal. The one gives and the other takes. The giving is the feminine principle (*anima*); it is a passivity, with the urge to surrender and sacrifice even unto death and extinction, which modern psychologists describe in terms of the unconscious or the libido. The other is the masculine principle (*animus*) with the urge to self-preservation; it is dominating and assertive. *Anima* is the passionate urge that drives one to get involved and lose oneself; *animus* is the urge to preserve one's identity. The heart is dominant in *anima*; the mind is dominant in *animus*.[16]

These two aspects of love – the self-sacrificing and the self-regarding are found in every human being, with one usually predominant. Personality is governed by the interplay of these two aspects of love.

It is by the power of *Agapē* (the distinctive word used for love in the New Testament) that a balance between the two is maintained; it is in *Agapē* that the perfect correspondence between the two can be found. For God is Love, and His love was perfectly demonstrated in the sacrifice of Jesus Christ, in which He gave all without reserve, making Himself nothing,[17] and in which He received all without change.[18] The centrifugal and centripetal aspects of love were perfectly fulfilled in Him. Thus in love all is given without reserve and all is received without change.

It is by this *Agapē* of God in Christ that the *anima* and the *animus* in man are grasped and lifted to the dimension of the Spirit where the two are brought into a perfect harmony. This harmony of the two is implied in the command: 'Love the Lord thy God with all thy heart, soul, mind and strength, and love thy neighbour as thyself.' To love God and the neighbour is the self-sacrificing love; to love the neighbour 'as thyself' is the self-regarding love.[19] When all is given to God all is received back from Him – 'He that loseth himself shall find himself.'

We can understand what this means in the light of the doctrine of the image already referred to. If man is made in the image of God, the more he loves God the more he perfects the image. The perfect love of God is the love of God for God's sake, without any tinge of self-love. In such a love the image conforms more and more to the likeness of God until it is perfected. This love does not begin with the self. In such love the self loses itself in God and in losing itself it finds itself. The image is thus perfected. Here the self-regarding love is perfected without any tinge of selfishness and the two loves are united in a perfect harmony. It is such a love alone that is capable of negating exclusive individuality and completing and fulfilling personality.

It is in this reciprocal love that self-loss becomes self-gain and that 'death is swallowed up in victory.'[20] In the relationship of mutual love no one dies; one lives in the other's love. 'We know that we have passed out of death into life, because we love the brethren.'[21] 'Nothing can separate us from the love of Christ . . . '[22] In love we participate in that which does not pass away; 'Love never ends.'[23] In other words love is eternal because God is Love. Every act of love, whether it be in the form of the husband's love for his wife, the mother's love for her children, the concern for human rights and justice and self-giving service, is a sacrament of eternal life. Love is undergirded by eternity.

Because love on the one hand implies the total surrender of self (centrifugal love), in the final state exclusive individuality will be completely negated. Self-contained, self-conscious individuality disappears. Centrifugal love therefore leads to the extinction of the self – the dying-out of separate individuality. We could therefore speak of this goal as *Nirvāna*. In the end we cease completely to be individuals. In love, *taṇhā* (craving) and the notion of I-ness which is at the basis of *taṇhā* are conquered. Christianity therefore does not fall into the error of eternalism (*sassata diṭṭhi*).

On the other hand, to speak of total self-negation would amount to nihilism (*uccheda diṭṭhi*). However, centripetal love overcomes this contradiction. This quality of love perfects personality in the end.

Love is neither union nor absorption, but communion. In communion, love integrates being with being and being with Being. There is a perfect integration of the self with the eternal in which individuality disappears. Here is the Hindu quest for union or absorption and the Buddhist quest for self-negation. But since in communion, love differentiates, personal identity is preserved within a totality. It is not an identity in the sense of a solitary self-contained entity, but a recognisability in a relationship, for a person can be recognised as a person only as he is known in a relationship. This principle of integration and differentiation is at the basis of the two-fold movement of love and is of great significance for our understanding of the final state of being, which is neither absorption nor separation, neither eternalism nor nihilism.

The experience of this final blessedness is not something that comes after death. It is an experience that can be enjoyed here and now. It is in love that one has a foretaste of the life that is to be. It is in love that we experience daily in some measure the negation of exclusive individuality and the fulfilment of personality. The life of love is a life of mutual giving and receiving, of individualisation and participation, of self-loss and self-gain, in which all is given without reserve and all is received without loss. A very human analogy, already alluded to, is that of lovers, who, the more they are lost in each other, the more they realise themselves. And this is an experience that we have all around us, in marriage, in friendship or in service. Thus the destiny of man is intimately related to the nature of man; man grows towards the End. What man is essentially he becomes finally. His essential nature is perfected through progressive sanctification here and in the hereafter until all things reach their consummation in the Kingdom, when God will be all in all.

D.T. Niles has an illuminating passage which more or less sums up our main thought:

> The nature of personality must be the clue to our understanding of the nature of life after death. When a child is born into the world, it is born an individual, but, by the very fact that it comes attached to its mother, it possesses the seed of personality. This growth in personality begins straightaway. Personal relationship is established between the child and its mother, the child and its nurse, the child and its father, and so on. As the child grows it becomes more and more of a person and less and less of an individual. Personality consists in the range, variety and depth of our relationships. It is the operation of the 'image' relation which is the basic factor in human personality. In heaven we shall be fully persons and cease completely to be individuals. We shall retain our differentiation as persons, without that differentiation being expressed in the exclusiveness of individuality. We shall retain personal identity within a complete harmony. The relationship on earth will be fulfilled in heaven, except that the implications of exclusiveness in those will have ceased to have meaning. An illuminating example is in the teaching of Jesus with respect to the most exclusive of human relationships–'When they shall rise from the dead, they neither marry nor are given in marriage, but are as the angels which are in heaven' (Matt: 22:30). There is only one marriage relationship there, that of the Lamb to his bride.[24]

Personality consists, not in an immortal entity within man, but in the 'range, variety and depth of our relationships'. To be is to be related. A person exists in a personal-communal relationship.

This relationship consists in the interplay of individualisation and participation which are interdependent on all levels of life. Through individualisation and participation, the I and the Thou meet inherently in union and distinction.

The personal-communal nature of personality is the clue to our understanding of the nature of life here and in the hereafter. Personality grows in the communion of personal encounter and is progressively sanctified in the hereafter until the goal is reached.

When individualisation reaches its perfect form which we call a 'person', participation reaches its perfect form which we call 'communion'. Neither reaches perfection apart from the other. Communion is not absorption into a distinctionless union, but is participation in which the person retains his differentiation as a person without the mark of exclusive individuality being expressed in it. The person loses his exclusiveness completely through participation but discovers his authentic selfhood through communion. The personal-communal relationship in which alone a person exists on earth will be perfected and fulfilled when all things reach final perfection in the Community of Love. John Macquarrie sees the end as 'a commonwealth of free responsible beings united in love; and this great end is possible only if finite existents are preserved in some kind of individual identity.'[25] It must be emphasised that the highest love is not a drive toward union, but rather communion, in which individual identity of some kind is preserved within a harmony, without the implications of exclusiveness.

Here we can find a satisfactory solution to the problem of the quest for self-identity which does not fall into the errors of either nihilism or eternalism. Since the person exists only in participation and not by an intrinsic potentiality, there is no question of eternalism; and since the person retains a differentiation in communion, there is no question of nihilism. But such an understanding is possible only if we accept the reality of God, with whom a person can enter into communion. It is now necessary for us to examine this much misunderstood concept of God and see its importance in relation to the doctrine of *anattā*, for an understanding of the solution to the problem of the self.

13 Anattā and God

At a time when there is so much 'God-talk', I believe that a biblical understanding of *anattā* can deepen our understanding of what the term 'God' means. It is my contention that, if *anattā* is real, God is necessary; it is in relation to the Reality of God that the reality of *anattā* can be meaningful. Because man is *anattā*, God is indispensable; because man is absolutely *anattā* God is absolutely necessary. The conditioned (*saṃkhata*) man has nothing to hope for unless there is an Unconditioned Reality (*asaṃkhata*). It is in relation to the Unconditioned (God) that the full depth and significance of *anattā* can be understood.

To assert that man has within himself the intrinsic self-derived power to transcend conditioned existence is to deny the full import of *anattā*. If man can save himself, *anattā* is not real. Christianity takes the meaning of *anattā* in all its seriousness and denies any form of intrinsic power in man – be it karmic force or the power of mind, *viññāṇa* – by which he can save himself. The substitution of a dynamic concept of the self (*viññāṇa santati*) for a static one does not remove the difficulty. For Christianity *anattā* means *anattā* in its fullest sense. As Karl Barth puts it, 'Man without God is not; he is neither being nor existence'.[1] Barth goes on to say that man is

> in no case so made that he is simply there, as though self-grounded, self-based, self-constituted and self-maintained. His constitution is in no case that of first and last reality; nor is it one which enables and empowers him to understand himself by himself, or to hold the criteria of his own perception and thought, however he may define them, as standards by the help of which he can, secluded in himself, arrive at the core of the matter. As he is not without God, he cannot understand himself without God.[2]

It is important to underline the truth that man cannot understand himself by himself or find the criterion of self-understanding within himself. Existence does not provide the key to existence. There is no human solution to the human problem.

As the Calvinist axiom has it, 'The finite is not capable of the infinite' (*finitum non capax infiniti*). The Christian assertion is that 'man exists as he is grounded, constituted and maintained by God.'[3] Therefore, 'He must and would perish immediately, hopelessly and eternally, if God ceased to be for him the living God, from whom he may expect that he will continually act on him accordingly.'[4]

2. LIGHT FROM THE UDĀNA PASSAGE

To explain what this means we could employ the famous Udāna passage in the Pātaligama Vagga of the *Khuddaka Nikāya*:

> Monks, there is [*atthi*] a not-born [*ajātaṃ*], a not-become [*abhūtaṃ*], a not-made [*akataṃ*], a not-compounded [*asaṃ-khataṃ*]. If that unborn, not-become, not-made, not-compounded were not, there would be apparent no escape from this here that is born, become, made, compounded. But since, monks, there is an unborn, unbecome, unmade, uncompounded, therefore is apparent the escape from this here that is born, become, made, compounded.[5]

The implication underlying this passage is that the Unconditioned Reality is indispensable if man is to escape the conditioned; apart from the Unconditioned there can be no escape for that which is conditioned. To put it in another way: if man is absolutely *anattā* the hypothesis of the Unconditioned or some such other hypothesis becomes absolutely necessary if the error of nihilism (*ucchedadiṭṭhi*) is to be avoided. Apart from the Unconditioned Reality there can be no emancipation for that which is conditioned; all that can be expected is total annihilation. One is therefore not surprised that Gunapala Dharmasiri, in dispensing with the idea of God, has completely extinguished Nirvāna.[6] In *A Buddhist Critique of the Christian concept of God*, Dharmasiri has weighed the merits of the Buddhist doctrine of *anattā* against the so-called Christian concept of the immortal soul. Rejecting the idea of the immortal soul, he affirms the doctrine of *anattā*, according to which a person is 'a conglomeration of psychic factors'[7] and nothing more. Personal identity and moral responsibility, he claims, 'can be explained in terms of the memory and the causal continuity of the process involved'.[8] This process ultimately leads to Nirvāna, which according to Dharmasiri is 'complete extinction'. Explaining this, he says that the Buddha used the term Nirvāna 'in the sense of complete extinction'.[9]

If his contention that *Nirvāna* is complete extinction is correct, then of course God, or the Ultimate Reality, is not necessary. On the other hand, if extinction is not the final end, the Ultimate Reality becomes necessary. This is because finitude — the realm of the born, the become, the made, the compounded — cannot contain by its own intrinsic power the reality that negates and transcends finitude. We need not dispute the fact that within this fathom-long body is the malady as well as the remedy; but the remedy is what is 'given' and not self-derived. Man himself, being in his totality the malady, cannot produce the remedy, just as a cancer cannot produce its own cure.

The Udāna passage under consideration has been interpreted by scholars in a negative as well as a positive sense. Dharmasiri, in keeping with his theory that *Nirvāna* indicates an 'experience' of complete extinction, takes it in the negative sense and argues that the contrasting epithets in this passage only emphasise the marked difference between *samsāra* (the phenomenal cycle of existence) and *Nirvāna* and should not be taken in a descriptive sense.[10] Traditionally, however, the epithets 'Unborn', 'Uncreated', etc., have been taken to refer to *Nirvāna* in a positive sense. Scholars are however of divided opinion as to whether these epithets refer to *Nirvāna* as the Absolute or to an Absolute Reality beyond *Nirvāna*. Some[11] argue that if *Nirvāna* is conceived as the cessation of desire it would be dependent on a psychological state and therefore could not exist prior to it. If *Nirvāna* is an experience of self-negation resulting from the extinction of desire it cannot exist separately. Therefore the epithets 'Unborn', 'Uncreated', etc., cannot in the strict sense be applied to *Nirvāna*.

There are others who think that these epithets refer to an Absolute Reality distinct from *Nirvāna*. It is a Reality that is (*atthi*). E. R. Sarathchandra, who interprets the Buddha's solution to man's problem in a purely existential, practical and personal way, ruling out the idea that the Buddha believed in an Absolute Reality, nevertheless refers to the Udāna passage as the only one isolated utterance which might lead to an interpretation 'that the Buddha placed an uncaused absolute reality against the fleeting reality of the phenomenal world as did the *Vedānta*.'[12] As a matter of fact this passage has lent itself to such an interpretation.

Nāgārjuna, making a specific reference to this Udāna passage, emphatically states that without the acceptance of the Ultimate Reality (*Paramārtha*) there can be no deliverance (*Nirvāna*) from conditioned existence (*Paramārtham anāgamya nirvānam nādhigamyate*).[13]

It is clear that Nāgārjuna makes a distinction between the *Paramārtha* and *Nirvāna*. According to him the attainment to the state of *Nirvāna* is possible because there is an Ultimate Reality (*Paramārtha*). *Nirvāna* is an experience related to the Absolute and is not the Absolute in itself. It is in this sense that I have used the term *Nirvāna* and attempted to understand it from a Christian point of view.

D. C. Wijewardana, referring to the above Udāna passage and other passages, says that they 'really refer to the Ultimate Reality and have probably been borrowed from the expressions applied to Brahman in the Upanishads.'[14] Oldenberg also recognises the similarity between the expressions used in the Udāna passage and those applied to Brahman, although he gives a different interpretation. 'These words', he says, 'seem to sound as if we heard Brahmanical philosophers talking of the Brahman, the unborn, intransient, which is neither great nor small, the name of which is 'No, No'; for no words can exhaust his being.'[15] There is indeed a passage in the *Kathā Upanishad* which seems to have influenced the Udāna passage:

> The Intelligent Self is neither born [*na jāyate*] nor does it die. It did not originate from anything [*na kutascit*] nor did anything originate from it [*na babhuva*]. It is Unborn [*ajah*], eternal [*nityah*], undecaying [*sāsvatah*] and Primeval [*purānah*].[16]

The similarity of the expressions here to those in the Udāna passage is striking. This way of speaking about the Ultimate Reality is congenial to the Indian mind, and there is some reason to suppose that the Buddha, a son of India, or later Buddhist thinkers (the Udāna was a later work) were influenced by such Upanishadic passages and that they used those epithets in the Udāna to refer to an Ultimate Reality other than *Nirvāna*.

Oldenberg holds the view that 'For the Buddhist the words "there is an uncreated" merely signify that the created can free himself from the curse of being created – there is a path from the World of the created out into dark endlessness.' The question then arises: 'Does the path lead into a new existence? Does it lead into Nothing?' Oldenberg's answer probably voices the Theravāda position. He says,

> The Buddhist creed rests in a delicate equipoise between the two. *The longing of the heart that craves the eternal has not nothing, and yet the thought has not a something which it might firmly grasp.* Further off the idea of the endless, the eternal, could not withdraw itself from belief than it has done here, where, like a gentle flutter on the point of merging in the Nothing, it threatens to evade the gaze.[17]

The words I have italicised are very significant. If I understand these words correctly, they mean that the longing of the heart for the eternal hits something and not nothing, but that that something is a reality apprehended in religious experience which surpasses the human mind and speech to grasp, define and describe. If this can be regarded as the Buddhist approach to reality, then there is much that Christians can learn from it.

3. THE SUPRA-DEPTH LEVEL OF ULTIMACY

Perhaps the greatest obstacle to belief in God is that we seem to know too much about Him, to the point that God ceases to be God. Christian theology has put God under a microscope and has sought minutely to analyse Him, and the resulting theologies, theories, and conceptual formulations (most of which are inventions of a western culture and not truly biblical) have obscured our vision of Reality.

We must guard against thinking that we can understand God by theories and conceptual formulations. St Paul wrote, 'O the depth of the riches and wisdom and knowledge of God! How unsearchable are his judgements and how inscrutable his ways! For from him and through him and to him are all things; to him be glory for ever.'[18] The realisation that the utmost knowledge we can have of God is to recognise his utter ineffability and incomprehensibility evokes adoration and silent contemplation – 'to him be glory for ever'. Our theologies have robbed us of this spiritual dimension.

We need to turn away from our notions of God which hide Him, to an understanding of ourselves so that we may find Him in the depth of being. God is really known in the abyss of one's being, in the realisation that one is *anattā* and therefore cannot depend on oneself for one's salvation. To reach that point, one has to pass through the dark night of the soul; through the desert where God Himself has forsaken one. In one of his most elusive and profound statements Paul Tillich says, 'The courage to be, is rooted in the God who appears when God has disappeared in the anxiety of doubt.'[19] It is in the abyss of being – the discovery that one is born, created, made, compounded, and nothing more; an emptiness of soul and even absence of God – that one discovers a Reality – an Unborn, an Unbecome, an Unmade and an Uncompounded – that transcends being. It is the discovery of emptiness – that man is but dust and to dust he shall return – that can annihilate self, and in the annihilation of self, one is led to the discovery of the oneness of emptiness and fullness. When man realises that he is *natthi* (nothing) in himself, he discovers that, he is in fact *atthi* in the abyss of his being.

In *Jesus Rediscovered* Malcolm Muggeridge (who 'never wanted God, or feared a God, or felt under any necessity to invent one' but was 'driven to the conclusion that God wants me'[20]) has some very pertinent things to say. Speaking of the sense of oneness that results from the experience of confronting God, he says, 'This sense of oneness, with the consequent release from the burden of the self, I take to be God—something which indubitably exists, which not only has not died, but cannot die.'[21] This something, he says, is the living God:

A being with whom one has relationship, on the one hand, inconceivably more personal than the most intimate human one, to the point that, as we are told, God has actually counted the hairs of each head; on the other, so remote that in order to establish a valid relationship at all, it is necessary to die, to murder one's own flesh with the utmost ferocity, and batter down one's ego as one might a deadly snake, a cobra which has lifted its hooded head with darting forked tongue to sting. (I say 'a being', which suggests a person, a spirit, a genie coming out of a bottle, and so is utterly inappropriate. There are no adequate words for any of the great absolutes, like life and death, good and evil; only for trivialities like politics and economics and science. One falls back on the meaningless monosyllable, God, as Hindu *sadhus* in their spiritual exercises endlessly repeat the equally meaningless monosyllable, Oom.)[22]

To put this in Buddhist terms: in order to establish a relationship with the Not-born, Not-become, Not-made, Not-compounded, it is necessary to die, to be released from the burden of the self, to realise that one is born, become, made and compounded and as such is *anattā*. This I take it, is what *Nirvāna* means – the extinction of the ego. Thus, echoing Malcolm Muggeridge, we could say that the sense of oneness, of communion with Reality, a relationship with the Transcendent, consequent on the release from the burden of the self, is the experience of God. This is an experience in which one realises that there is a Reality which goes beyond the level of rational thinking to a supra-depth level of Ultimacy – what one might call the realm of the *Avyākata*. Intimations of that Ultimacy, of that Transcendent, are found in everyday experience. Even in the midst of suffering and evil, the sense of good and bad and of what ought and ought not to be, or, in other words, the sense of value, is an indication of value in an ultimate sense. The encounter with *dukkha*, as in the case of Prince Siddhārtha, creates within man a transformative urge towards the Ultimate. That urge itself is a pointing to the Ultimate Reality.

To quote Whitehead, there has always been, consciously or unconsciously, an intuition, a feeling, a vision

of something which stands beyond, behind, and within, the passing flux of immediate things; something that is real, and yet waiting to be realized; something which is a remote possibility, and yet the greatest of present facts; something that gives meaning to all that passes, and yet eludes apprehension; something whose possession is the final good, and yet is beyond all reach; something which is the ultimate ideal, and the hopeless quest.[23]

The term God is used to signify this 'Something'. There has never been and never will be a completely satisfactory concept of this 'Something' which Christians call God. But there has always been and always will be a reaching out of the mind for a worthier and greater concept of God. That reaching out, that quest, expressed particularly in worship, is itself a significant aspect of man's experience of God, in his pilgrimage towards that ultimate goal – the Kingdom of God, the Community of Love.

If man is really *anattā*, God is indispensable for his salvation. If God is not, then *anattā* necessarily implies final extinction. If God is, then the realisation that one is *anattā* leads to the experience of emptiness and fullness (*suññatā-puṇṇatā, natthi-atthi, anattā-pneuma*) all in one.

In the ultimate sense, this experience, so far as we can infer from our understanding of the *anattā-pneuma* nature of man, means the giving of one's deepest to that Ultimate Reality, whose depth has no end.

14 The Practical Relevance of the Anattā-pneuma Concept

What is the significance of our understanding of man in terms of *Anattā-pneuma* for a socially relevant ethic? Is the study of man just an academic subject or one of mere religious or philosophical interest? Has it any bearing on the present-day man's search for community? Has it anything to say in an age of science and technology when many people, particularly the young, are turning away from traditional forms of religion? I am convinced that our study, though it has been largely academic, can contribute much to the search for authentic selfhood and community, in which Marxists, Maoists and followers of other secular ideologies are as much involved as theologians and philosophers, mystics and hippies.

I. THE SEARCH FOR COMMUNITY

I believe that to make meaning of religion today, it is essential that we recognise the fact that the modern world is moving towards a global unity and that mankind is seeking for a kind of community in which people can live together with their seriously different traditions and truth claims in peace, mutual trust and co-operation.

Signs of an emerging world community are seen all around us. The Middle-East war of 1973 has brought home to us, as never before in human history, the degree of our interdependence and our need of one another. Technology, by making possible hitherto unheard-of speed in communication and travel, has made every person into every other person's neighbour. All crucial problems are world problems and hardly anything of importance can happen even in a remote corner of the world which does not concern all.

Thus a single destiny governs the whole world and the emerging world community can already be observed in embryo.

There is no doubt that religious teachers, prophets and seers of the past had such a vision of world community. For the Buddha, *Dhamma* meant that which belongs to humanity as a whole, and he sought to bring about a community — the *Sangha* — free from caste distinctions and priestly control. For Jesus Christ the Kingdom of God meant the universal community of love where there is neither 'Jew nor Greek, bond nor free, male nor female'.[1] For the Prophet Muhammad *Umma* meant a fellowship of believers which transcends racial and communal barriers. For Karl Marx, the 'Classless Society' meant a down-to-earth concept of community realisable in human history. They all had a global outlook, which unfortunately was lost as religions and ideologies developed in historical, cultural and political circumstances in isolation from one another, having distinguishing and discriminating labels. The time has come for people of different faiths to look beyond labelled religion to global religion, from insular communities to world community.

This means that we should not regard the religious life of man as enveloped in mutually exclusive systems, but as dimensions of a universal spirituality; we need to adopt a catholic humanitarian world view recognising and appreciating spiritual experience in its various manifestations; we need to realise that the convergence of all spiritual traditions is essential to the future well-being of man and society.

This does not mean the absorption of all world religions into one world religion. It is not a 'fruit-salad of religions' nor is it a super-religion over and above all other religions, producing one religion for one world. The one world community will be typified not by uniformity but by unity as well as diversity; cultural and religious differences and diversities will continue, but the relation between them may resemble the different denominations within Christianity or the sects in Buddhism (taking Mahāyāna also into account) with the growing understanding already manifest reaching a greater degree of resonance. This means that each religion must reflect within its community of faith the global outlook in its own particular form, being true to the spirit of its own teachings. No basic truths in any religion need to be watered down or compromised with. However, it would be necessary to look at them with critical eyes and reconceive and reinterpret them to meet the growing demands of world community. In other words labelled religions must have a global outlook if they are to play a community-creating role. The intensity and vitality of religions in their particular forms must be power-cells, not ghettos in community. It is only in this way that religious truths can be revitalised and religions can become relevant in a world which appears to have discarded them.

2.   LIGHT FROM THE NEW SCIENTIFIC CONSCIOUSNESS

Contemporary scientific thinking has arrived at a revolutionary conception of matter, which contradicts the traditional notion that matter consists of indestructible unchangeable autonomous atoms. Table salt for instance was considered to be a particular form of matter made up of an atom of sodium and an atom of chlorine, each being a bit of the cosmic stuff called sodium and chlorine. However, explorations into the micro-world within the atom have revealed the remarkable insight that the most fundamental realities of matter, as Harold K. Schilling puts it, 'are relationships, processes, and events rather than bits of substance'.[2] 'Thus man has become keenly conscious', Schilling continues, 'that fundamentally *matter is relational*, much more like a delicate fabric of dynamic inter-relationships than an edifice of hard building blocks.'[3]

Within this relationality of matter, as Schilling points out, there are two other exceedingly interesting qualities. Firstly, *gregariousness*, i.e., the tendency of 'elementary particles' to congregate or unite, to come together and stay together and form into larger and more complex structures. Secondly, apart from mere coming together and staying together, there is also building together; matter is seen to display remarkable developmental drives; it is constructive, it builds. Therefore there is an *evolution* not only of the biological species but also of inanimate matter itself. To begin with there were elementary particles or atoms of the simplest kind, namely, those of hydrogen; later, different species of atoms and of molecules came on the scene; and still later, combinations of molecules, such as crystals and rocks, rivers and oceans, planets and galaxies. Thus we see that in inanimate matter there has been a dynamism, a developmental drive, an evolution from the simple to the complex.

This new insight into the nature of matter has brought about a change in the vocabulary and language employed in talking about it. The interest now is not in the location or shape of the electron but in 'the pitch or the note it is singing'; not in the space-relations of electrons but in their harmonic relations with other electrons; not in their motion but in their music; not in drawing a diagram to show the location of an electron but 'in writing the music of its song'.[4] The language now employed in speaking about matter is not particle language but music language. As Schilling puts it:

> Contemporary man can now sense the symphonic character of physical reality and hear metaphorically the music of the spheres within the atom. He is now far more fascinated by the melodic quality and dynamism of its singing than in the blueprints of its mechanical character.[5]

This insight into the nature of matter gives us a new understanding of the universe, that it is not materialistic but *relational*. If this is true of the material world, how much more true it is of the world of persons-in-relation. The material world itself is a testimony to the fact that the highest values are relational values which can best be realised in communally integrated living. Just as molecules join together to constitute a biological cell or a physical crystal, forming an organised integrated entity, so individuals, men and women, are related to one another in a communally integrated entity – a new humanity.

This does not however mean that the individual loses his significance as an individual by being integrated into a community. As science now sees it, the molecules that constitute a crystal are not absorbed into the crystal but are active and dynamic; they contribute to the symphony of the whole. Similarly an individual person has a dynamic role to play in the community. As a cell, for instance, or a crystal joins with other cells or crystals and so on to form larger integrated entities, so organised communities join with other communities to form a larger community entity.

Thus physical science provides a picture of an overall integrated community. It gives us a picture of what the Community of Love, the Kingdom of God, will look like – a societal organism in which the I and the Thou meet inherently in union and distinction, wherein individuals can be themselves in the most meaningful way. This new science, particularly the evolutionary character of inanimate matter, points to the emergence or developmental drive towards integrated humanity – the world community – which is what secular ideologies are also striving for.

3. IDEOLOGICAL DIMENSIONS IN THE SEARCH FOR COMMUNITY

(a) The socialist man

There is much that religion and secular ideologies can learn from one another. 'Secularity serves religion', says Raymond Pannikar, 'by guarding it from unreality, and religion serves secularity by guarding it from being inhuman.'[6] Both have a complementary role to play.

Secular ideologies have stressed the social character of man. Karl Marx, who was very much influenced by Feuerbach, says:

> Feuerbach resolves the religious essence into the human essence. But the human essence is no abstraction inherent in each single individual. In its reality it is the ensemble of social relations.[7]

The important concept Feuerbach uses in this connection is 'species-being'. The species is the real being; the individual is simply a particular instance of the life of the species. Martin Buber considers this discovery of man's real being as the most significant contribution of Feuerbach. He calls it the Copernican revolution of modern thought and quotes the following words of Feuerbach:

> The individual man for himself does not have man's being in himself, either as a moral being or a thinking being. Man's being is contained only in community, in the unity of man with man—a unity which rests, however, only in the reality of the difference between I and Thou.[8]

In *Das Kapital* Marx expresses this idea as follows:

> Since the human being does not come into the world bringing a mirror with him, not yet a Fichtean philosopher able to say 'I am myself', he first recognizes himself as reflected in other men. The man Peter grasps his relation to himself as a human being through becoming aware of his relation to the man Paul as a being of like mind with himself. Thereupon Paul, with flesh and bone, with all his Pauline corporeality, becomes Peter the phenomenal form of mankind.[9]

This is a truth we have stressed throughout in our study of the biblical view of man. It is one aspect of what we mean by *pneuma* – the fact that man is by nature communal, that to *be* is to be related. Man's true humanity is relationality or mutuality.

In the above quotation as well as elsewhere, Marx affirms that man's real existence is social existence and the goal of man is his regaining of self in a communist society. But man is far from this goal because his present existence is marked by alienation. Alienation is a fundamental concept in Marx's understanding of the nature of man. Alienation for Marx appears in three forms: (*a*) alienation from the object of one's labour; (*b*) alienation of labour from the act of production – self-alienation; and (*c*) alienation of man from man. The goal is the annulment of this alienation, which will result in a classless society.

Alienation is a concept used in both existentialist philosophy and depth psychology. The picture that emerges from these disciplines is that of a man, a stranger to himself, bound by the chains of his own making and struggling to free himself from this bondage. Christian theologians have seen the connection between this concept of alienation and the biblical concept of sin; one might even see its connection with the Buddhist concept of *dukkha*. This is a word which means disharmony, conflict, unsatisfactoriness, anxiety, etc., a word which describes the predicament in which man is, in his state of alienation.

Another term, namely *anomie*, is used by sociologists to indicate this predicament in which man is.[10] This concept was initially developed by Emile Durkheim in *Le Suicide* to signify a condition of normlessness in a society or group. Although it refers to a state of rulelessness or deregulation in the social sphere it is, by extension, applied to individuals too. As Durkheim has pointed out, anomic suicide is common among individuals who lack self-identity with a community or system of values or norms; it therefore refers to uprooted man in search of self-identity and community.

Marx's humanism was generic rather than personal; the overcoming of alienation is therefore a collective human achievement. In Marx's view it is collective man who could dominate nature and overcome all obstacles to 'free conscious activity'. Religion is an obstacle to this revolutionary freedom because it provides 'pie in the sky when you die', which dulls man's will to work for social change. However, gruesome inhumanities which have gone hand-in-hand with the enthronement of collective human achievement, in which the individual can be so eclipsed as to lose his freedom, have in the post-Stalin era in Russia and Eastern Europe revealed that human nature is not simply the product of social existence, but has a deeper personal dimension. It is being increasingly recognised that without a revolution within there can be no revolution without. Even the great Cuban revolutionary Che Guevara recognised this truth. It is said that his whole outlook was governed by one fundamental principle: 'that no matter how much you change a society, no matter how much you restructure it, unless you create a new man, unless you change his attitudes, it all ends up in *greed, lust* and *ambition*.'[11] The same truth is expressed in a statement which outlines the purposes of UNESCO: 'Since wars begin in the minds of men, it is in the minds of men that the defence of peace must be constructed.'

(b) The selfless man

It is at this point that the relevance of religion can best be seen. To create the new man you must strike at the root cause of '*greed*', '*lust*' and '*ambition*', or in Buddhist terms, *lobha* (greed) *dosa* (hatred) and *moha* (delusion). More simply stated, the root cause of all evil is *taṇhā*; it is primarily the thirst for self. Therefore, we could say that it is by self-emptying, by realising the truth of *anattā*, that the new man can come into being.

Selflessness is a great virtue that Chairman Mao Tse-tung ceaselessly upheld and exemplified in his life. The new person that the revolutionary struggles in the People's Republic of China try to create is primarily a selfless person. Mao, paying a warm-hearted tribute to one of his comrades on his death, said:

> Comrade Bethune's spirit, his utter devotion to others without any thought of self, was shown in his boundless sense of responsibility in his work and boundless warm-heartedness towards all comrades and people. Every communist must learn from him. . . . We must all learn the spirit of absolute selflessness from him. With this spirit everyone can be very useful to the people. A man's ability may be great or small, but if he has this spirit, he is already noble-minded and pure, a man of moral integrity and above vulgar interests, a man who is a value to the people.

In this passage the relation between absolute selflessness and social responsibility comes out very clearly. It is the selfless man who truly knows and fulfils his social responsibilities. The realisation of the truth of *anattā* and the realisation of social goals are therefore seen to be interrelated.

Seeing that there was a tendency towards selfish departmentalism among some members in his party, he said:

> We must intensify our effort to educate such persons and to make them understand that selfish departmentalism is a sectarian tendency which will become very dangerous if allowed to develop.

He commends selflessness as the noblest quality in a Communist:

> At no time and in no circumstances should a Communist place his personal interests first; he should subordinate them to the interests of the nation and of the masses. Hence, selfishness, slacking, corruption, seeking the limelight, and so on, are most contemptible, while selflessness, working with all one's energy, whole-hearted devotion to public duty, and quiet hard work will command respect.

He condemns everything that inflames the ego, the self:

> A Communist must never be opinionated or domineering, thinking that he is good in everything while others are good in nothing; he must never shut himself up in his little room, or brag and boast and lord it over others.[12]

There is something religious in these 'Thoughts' of Mao. Has not religion something to contribute to create that kind of selfless man? It certainly has and can do much if it orientates itself to the needs of the people, both spiritual and physical. There is a religious dimension in man which makes religion of some sort necessary for him.

(c) The transcendent man

Pandit Jawaharlal Nehru, committed more or less dogmatically to the creed of scientific humanism, which he shared with many of his student generation of Cambridge, was intensely conscious of the

need of man to go beyond himself so that he reached a spiritual
dimension of life. In a conversation with a journalist he said:

> I do not happen to be a religious man, but I do believe in
> something—call it religion or anything you like—which raises
> man above his normal level and gives the human personality a
> new dimension of spiritual quality and moral depth. Now,
> whatever helps to raise a man above himself, be it some god or
> even a stone image, is good. Obviously it is a good thing and must
> not be discouraged. Speaking for myself, my religion is tolerance
> of all religions, creeds and philosophies.

The journalist further asked him about the problem created by
science and technology. Nehru's reply and the conversation that
followed reveal certain aspects of his 'religion':

> Nehru: I wonder if a problem like this can be tackled scientifi-
> cally to the exclusion of other values. What appears to be wanting
> is—I do not know how to put it—except to say that it is an ethical
> aspect, which might be wanting some spiritual solution.
> Journalist: Is not that unlike the Jawaharlal of yesterday, Mr.
> Nehru, to talk in terms of ethical and spiritual solutions? What
> you say raises visions of Mr. Nehru in search of God in the evening
> of his life.
> N: If you put it that way, my answer is 'Yes'. I have changed.
> The emphasis on ethical and spiritual solutions is not uncon-
> scious. It is deliberate, quite deliberate. There are good reasons
> for it. First of all, apart from material development that is
> imperative, I believe that the human mind is hungry for
> something deeper in terms of moral and spiritual development,
> without which all the material advance may not be worth
> while . . .
>   The problem is that once a person's physical wants are
> satisfied—that is, he's got enough money, employment, a home
> and other essentials—then he ceases to have a sure function of life.
> J: He gets engulfed in a spiritual vacuum?
> N: Yes, a spiritual vacuum, an emptiness of the spirit, the result
> of which is what you call the angry young men and women of our
> generation.[13]

Nehru speaks of a 'new dimension of spiritual quality' which 'helps to raise a man above himself'. This spiritual quality is what we have called *pneuma*, particularly that aspect of transcendence. But one cannot go beyond oneself without in some measure realising that one is *anattā*.

We are witnessing the truth of what Nehru says in what is called the 'spiritual crisis of the post-Christian west'. In these countries, where Christianity has been preached for centuries, young people have moved away from the established churches and have turned to secular ideologies. However, many of them have become disenchanted with the values of a scientifically and technologically-oriented secular culture and are seeking to build up what Theodore Roszak calls 'a counter-culture'[14] in which they could find a meaningful way of life. A religious dimension — a new longing for transcendence — is a significant constituent of this counter-culture, as one could infer from the explorations into Eastern mysticism and occult practices that have increased amazingly in recent times. The spiritual vacuum (*anomie*), created by the secular culture has to a large extent been filled by spurious forms of religiosity. But they do not satisfy; they do not last. A system of values, a belief-system, a *Weltanschauung*, whether in the form of religion or ideology, must fill this anomic vacuum.

Religion with its other-worldly beliefs has failed to provide a satisfactory *Weltanschauung*. In the hands of exploiters, such other-worldly beliefs provide a convenient means of keeping the oppressed masses in subjection by holding out hopes of better life in heaven or in another birth in a heavenly world. Religion has thus become unreal. Therefore 'secularity serves religion by guarding it from unreality'.

On the other hand, this-worldly secular ideologies tend to make everything, including man, a means to an end. Man becomes dehumanised in this means-towards-end process. Therefore, 'religion serves secularity by guarding it from being inhuman.'

Is there a point at which these two approaches meet, correcting and supplementing each other?

Dietrich Bonhoeffer used the striking expression 'holy worldliness', by which he meant a simultaneous involvement in this world through participation in a reality that takes one beyond this world. As John Macquarrie interprets Bonhoeffer's thought, 'holy worldliness' means 'an acceptance of and an involvement in the world — this material world where God has been pleased to set us', and 'yet always there must be a searching below the surface of things for the holy depths that give meaning to this whole worldly existence and rescue it from pointlessness, if not indeed from sheer absurdity.'[15]

Religion would insist that to save the world from 'pointlessness' and 'absurdity' man must relate himself to a Reality that points to the Beyond from within. An exclusive concern for an earthly paradise makes man too much concerned with the world and himself. To be rightly related to this world, free from self-seeking, one must be sufficiently detached from the world. As Malcolm Muggeridge has put it: 'It is only the other-worldly who know how to cope with this world.'[16] But this other-worldliness or transcendence is not something beyond our reach but is the nearest thing to hand. As Bonhoeffer has put it, it is 'a new life for others, through participation in the being of God'.

4.   SPIRIT AND SPIRITUALITY

(a)   Meaning of spirituality

I have used the word spiritual without defining what this word means. Usually it suggests a kind of hot-house atmosphere where feelings and religious fervour run high. It is associated with emotion and devotion, ritual and worship. In an age dominated by science and technology this traditional meaning of the 'spiritual' is at stake. The meaning and relevance of the 'spiritual' is today raised anew by the so-called religions, and some have begun to speak about the 'spirituality of the secular' which challenges traditional notions of the 'spiritual.' Can we come to a common understanding?

Spirituality is embedded in and arises from the very nature of man; the fact that his true self is to be found not in the 'I' alone, because man is *anattā*, but in the 'I' and 'You', because man is *pneuma*. To be spiritual is to be truly human, and true humanness is non-egoistic relationality. In the light of the *anattā-pneuma* concept we could describe this spirituality as consisting of three spirit-qualities.

(b)   The three spirit-qualities

The first spirit-quality is *mutuality* or *right-relatedness*, that is, to be rightly related with one another, overcoming alienation of man from man. This is not simply having some nice feeling about one's neighbours and doing charitable deeds. The man who is rightly related is one who has a deep concern for social justice and the removal of those things that create distinctions between man and man. Thus, we could say that the concern of a Marxist for the abolition of class distinctions is a spiritual concern. Anything that is done to remove alienation of man from man, whether by the so-called religious men or by the so-called secular men, is spiritual. This understanding enables us to see morality in its right perspective, not as the observance of rigid absolute laws but as responsible living for the good of one another. Morality is not the adherence to inflexible absolute laws. Moral principles are situationally adaptable for responsible living for the common good of man. This is what it means to be a socialist man. In Christian terms this is what 'love thy neighbour' means.

The second spirit-quality can be called egolessness or anattā-ness; the realisation that one is nothing in oneself. One thereby overcomes the false notion of 'I', 'me' and 'mine' that stands in the way of right relationships.

To be rightly related to others one must be rightly related within, because the causes that separate man from man are within man himself. 'What causes war, and what causes fightings among you?', asks St James; 'Is it not your passions that are at war in your members? You desire and do not have; so you kill. And you covet and cannot obtain; so you fight and wage war.'[17] In one word it is selfishness or *taṇhā* and everything that promotes selfishness must be removed. Moral discipline towards this end is a dimension of spirituality.

Personal discipline is not primarily a way of saving one's soul but a way of attaining selflessness or anattā-ness in order that one may live relationally and not egoistically. It is from this point of view that the disciplines prescribed in the different religions must be looked at. The aim of discipline is to create the selfless man so that he can be the social man.

The third spirit-quality is transcendence. The word transcendence means to go beyond, as is clear from the etymology of the word – *trans* meaning across and *scandere* meaning to climb. Inborn in man there is a 'psychic aptitude' (to use Jung's phrase) for the beyond, for the transcendent. This inborn tendency is clearly seen in the growth of groups of people, particularly in the west, who, having discarded traditional religions, are turning to forms of Eastern spirituality such as *Yoga*, *Zen*, *Hare Krishna* and transcendental meditation.

There are some who think that transcendence is unrelated to life; it is something beyond, not within. But transcendence is a truly human quality which urges a person from within to go beyond himself. Therefore one must first look for transcendence within and not without. Transcendence is an everyday experience. Philip Wheelwright describes it as the *threshold experience*. Thus he says,

> Man always lives on the verge, always on the borderland of something more. He is the animal, apparently, who has built restlessness into a metaphysical principle. . . . Indeed the intimation of something more, beyond the horizon, belongs to the very nature of consciousness. To be conscious is not just to be; it is to mean, to intend, to point beyond oneself, to testify that some kind of beyond exists and to be ever on the verge of entering it.[18]

The love shining from the eyes of a bride, a scientist's devotion to his research, a mother's concern for her son, the haunting sweetness of music, the sense of wonder at the radiance of the sunset, the sense of immensity at the sight of the starry skies, the compulsions to reason and to question, the never-ceasing creative urge in man to create something new and higher and not remain satisfied with what is, the experience of nullity or anattā-ness which makes him realise that there is something beyond the born, the made, the created and the quest for meaning – these are all experiences that bring us to the threshold of something more. Even in atheism there is a dimension of transcendence, for atheism is a protest in the name of hope for the not-yet-comprehended.[19] Man inclines towards this something more in veneration, aspiration, hope and worship. In Marxism and other social ideologies, transcendence finds expression in faith-decisions made in hope oriented towards a glorious future; it creates a sense of glory. In religions this hope is oriented to a glorious future even beyond the grave. This also creates a sense of glory which finds expression in worship. In theistic religions transcendence is projected on to a personal God; in Buddhism on to the Buddha or the Dhamma as symbols of reality; in social ideologies it finds expression in personality cults. Some may need a concrete expression of the Transcendent, some may not; but no one can be human without a sense of transcendence. Transcendence is a summons from the Beyond that takes man beyond himself, by which alone he can discover authentic selfhood.

The spirit-quality of transcendence is in every man, whether he be a materialist, a Marxist, a Buddhist or a Christian. There is a beyond in science: the wonder and mystery of the immense range of depths in physical matter such as a grain of salt. There is a beyond in reason: an ever-receding something beyond the grasp of the mind — the inexplicable — what Buddhism calls *avyākata*. These point to an ultimate Beyond which gives meaning to the proximate beyonds — the experiences of transcendence in everyday life. Even after a hearty meal in a classless society there will still be a hunger for something MORE — for the BEYOND.

The search for world community urges us to seek for a form or forms of spirituality that can be shared by people of different faiths and ideologies. I have suggested that the basic criteria for such a spirituality can be derived from the understanding of spirituality in terms of *anattā-pneuma*. Religions have tended to emphasise inwardness (a characteristic particularly of renascent religions) to the neglect of social action, and ideologies have tended to emphasise social action to the neglect of inwardness. The understanding of spirituality in terms of *anattā-pneuma* will perhaps help participation in a common spirituality by linking inwardness with action, solitary contemplation with mutuality and transcendence with social involvement, because all these aspects are linked together in the very nature of man, characterised by the three qualities of mutuality, egolessness and transcendence. Anthropology, spirituality and sociology are thus seen to be interrelated.

Abbreviations

A.	Aṅguttara Nikāya
Brhd. Up.	Brihad-Āranyaka Upanishad
Chand. Up.	Chāndogya Upanishad
D.	Dīgha Nikāya
Dh. P.	Dhammapada
E.R.E.	Encyclopaedia of Religion and Ethics
M.	Majjhima Nikāya
Maitri Up.	Maitrī Upanishad
N.E.B.	New English Bible
P.T.S.	Pali Text Society
Ps.	Paṭisambhidāmagga
R.S.V.	Revised Standard Version of the Bible
S.B.B.	Sacred Books of the Buddhists
S.	Saṃyutta Nikāya
Sn.	Suttanipāta
Vinaya.	Vinaya Piṭaka
Vis } Vism }	Visuddhi Magga

References and Notes

2 Soul Theories

1. See 'Attan' in P.T.S. Pali-English Dictionary, (London: Luzac, 1959).
2. E.g. Rig Veda v. 58.
3. D. 1.31 mentions sixteen theories, D. 1.34 seven, and D. 1.186–7, three.
4. See A. L. Basham, *History and Doctrine of the Ajivakas* (London: Luzac, 1954).
5. Chand. Up. 6.8.6; 6.9.4; 6.12.3. (References are to R. E. Hume's *The Thirteen Principal Upanishads* (OUP, 1962.) What Hume translates as 'the finest essence' could be translated as 'the most minute'.
6. *Bhagavati Sutra*, xiii. 7.495.
7. 'There such a one goes around laughing, sporting, having enjoyment with women or chariots or friends, not remembering the appendage of this body. As a draft-animal is yoked in a wagon, even so this spirit (*prāṇa*) is yoked in this body.' (Chand. Up. 8.12.3, cf. Brhd. Up. 4.3.13.)
8. Brhd. Up. 2.1. 16–20; 4.3.9.
9. 'The Self (*ātman*) which is free from evil, ageless, deathless, sorrowless, hungerless, thirstless, whose desire is the Real, whose conception is the Real — He should be searched out, Him one should desire to understand. He obtains all worlds and all desires who has found out and who understands that Self.' (Chand. 8.7.1).
10. Brhd. Up. 4.3.13.
11. Chand. Up. 8.8.1; 3.13.8; 6.1.3; 6.16.3.
    Many centuries later, even the great philosopher Sankara, commenting on Brhd. Up. 4.5.6, believed that the ātman can be known through argument and reasoning (*tarkinopapattiya*).
12. Brhd. Up. 2.4.14. Matha. Up. 1.2.23. Mund. Up. 3.2.3.
13. Katha. Up. 1.3.12. Mund. Up. 3.1.8. cf. Katha. Up. 2.3.12; 1.2.23. Maitri. Up. 6.17.
14. Katha. Up. 2.18.19.
15. *Eastern Religions and Western Thought* (London: OUP, 1939) p. 83.
16. The allusion is to the idea of the 'net' in the *Brahmajala Sutta*.

3 The No-Soul Theory

1. *The Heart of Buddhist Meditation* (Colombo: M. D. Gunasena & Co., 1962) p. 35.
2. *Visuddhi Magga*, Ch. 18. H. C. Warren, *Buddhism in Translations* (Cambridge, Mass.: Harvard University Press, 1909) p. 185.
3. Ibid.
4. *Visuddhi Magga*, Ch. 18. Quoted by Nyānatiloka, *Buddhist Dictionary* (Colombo: Frewin & Co., 1956) p. 97.

5. *Process and Divinity*, p. 117.
6. S. 11.94. *The Book of Kindred Sayings – Saṃyutta Nikāya* – Part ii., tr. Mrs Rhys Davids (London: OUP, 1952) p. 66.
7. S. XII. 62. See Warren, op. cit., 151.
8. S. XXXV. 141.
9. S. XXI. 5.
10. S.XXII. 95.
    Both the above quotations are taken from Nyānatiloka, *Buddhist Dictionary*(Colombo: Frewin & Co., 1956) p. 73.
11. *Milindapañha*, 25.1. Warren, op. cit., pp. 129–33. (What appears above is an abridgement of this lengthy dialogue.)
12. S. III. 130.
13. S. XXII. 30.
14. Ibid. 29.
15. *What the Buddha Taught* (London: Gordon Frazer, 1959) p. 51.
16. *Mahāvagga* 1.6.38 as translated by Nārada Thera, *The Buddha and His Teachings* (Colombo: Vajirārāmaya, 1964) p. 100.
17. Ibid., pp. 100 – 1.
18. Ibid., pp. 101–2.
19. M. 1.128.
20. D. II. 156, tr. F. L. Woodward, *Some Sayings of the Buddha* (London: OUP, 1960) p. 356.
21. M. Sutta 13; A. IV. 136 f.
22. See M. Sutta 28; S. II. 191; A. IV. 100 ff.
23. S. II. 94–5.
24. S. XXII. 96.

4 *The Theravāda Point of View*

1. *Puggala Paññatti*, No. 141–5.
2. Dhammapada No. 294.
3. Dhammasaṅganī. 1315, 1316, 1319.
4. S. IV. 400–1.
5. *What the Buddha Taught*, op. cit., p. 66.
6. *Buddhist Analysis of Matter* (Ceylon: printed at the Government Press, 1967) p. 166.
7. S. III, p. 166; IV, p. 57.
8. Api Khvāham āvuso imasmiṃ yēva Vyāmatte Kaḷēvarē saññimhi samanake lokañca paññāpēmi lokasamudayañ ca lokanirodañ ca lokanirodhagāminiṃ paṭipada ca. (S. 1, 62. See also A. II, 48.)
9. *Buddhist Philosophy in India and Ceylon* Oxford: Clarendon Press, 1923) p. 56.
10. *Mahāvagga* IV. 100.
11. Ibid.
12. D. 17.
13. Ps. ii, 35–71; Vism. XXI, pp. 549–76. Also see Patisambhidāmagga II. 41, 42, 67 and Vism. XXII, 113, p. 597 for list of kinds of insight by which the truth of impermanency can be realised.
14. A. IV, 13–14. There are twelve *Anicca Suttas* all of which stress the

impermanency of the *Saṅkhāras*, S. III. 21, 22, 195, 199, 200; S. IV. 1.2–3, 4, 8.28; S.V. 214, 132.

15. The popular legend of the Great Renunciation is not found in the Pali canon. It is based on the story of the young noble named Yasa (*Vinaya* 1.7) and is expounded and embellished in the *Lalita Vistara* and the later *Commentary of the Jātaka Tales*.

16. *Zarathustra*, Pt. I. Chap. 9. quoted by Paul Tillich, *Courage to Be* (New York: Yale University Press, 1952) p. 27.

17. Ibid.

18. David E. Roberts, *Existentialism and Religious Belief* (New York: OUP, 1957) p. 17.

5 *The Problem of Self-identity*

1. 'On Nirvana, and on the Buddhist Doctrines of the "Groups", the Saṅkhāras, Karma and the "Paths"', *The Contemporary Review*, XXIX (1877) pp. 249–70.

2. Dhammapada 1 & 2.

3. M. i.373.

4. *Karma and Rebirth* (Ceylon: Buddhist Publication Society, n.d.), p. 2.

5. *The Path of Purity* (P.T.S., 1931) Vol. III. p. 665 f.

6. *Buddhist Psychology of Perception* (Colombo: University Press, 1958), pp. 80 and 82.

7. Vis. XIV. See Nyānatiloka, *Buddhist Dictionary*, op. cit., p. 30.

8. *Compendium of Philosophy*, a translation of the *Abhidhammattha-Sangaha* by Shwe Zan Aung; revised and edited by Mrs Rhys Davids, published for the Pali Text Society by Luzac & Co., (London, 1910; reprinted 1956 and 1963) pp. 11–12.

9. Ibid. p. 42.

10. I suspect that Hartshorne is better informed on Buddhism than Whitehead, partly because he has travelled quite a lot in Asia. Whitehead says he studied Buddhism 'very respectfully' in the 1920s, 'but I hadn't spent 20 years weighing up one theology to swallow another one whole' (L. Price, *Dialogues of A.N. Whitehead*, dialogue XXXV, p. 243).

11. Charles Hartshorne, *The Logic of Perfection and Other Essays in Neo-classical Metaphysics* (Chicago, Ill., Open Court Publishing Co., 1962), p. 18.

12. 'The Buddhist-Whiteheadian View of the Self and the Religious Traditions', *Proceedings of the Ninth International Congress of History of Religions*, p. 298.

13. *The Logic of Perfection*, p. 17

14. Einstein describes *events* as follows: 'In the pre-relativity physics, space and time were separate entities. Specifications of time were independent of the choice of the frame of reference. . . . One spoke of points of space as of instants of time, as if they were absolute realities. It was not observed that the true element of the space-time specification was the event specified by the four numbers (i.e. by four dimensions, three of space and one of time). . . . It is neither the point of space, nor the instant in time at which something happens that has physical reality, but only the event itself.' (A. Einstein, *The Meaning of Relativity*, p. 30.)

15. *Reality as Social Process* (Chicago, Ill.: The Free Press, 1953) p. 31.

16. Hartshorne and Reese, *Philosophers Speak of God*, p. 285.

17. *Proceedings of the Ninth International Congress for History of Religions*, op. cit., p. 301.

18. *Systematic Theology* (Chicago, Ill.: University of Chicago Press, 1950) Vol. I p. 181.

6 *The Quest for Self-Identity*

1. *Buddhist Thought in India* (London: Allen & Unwin, 1962) p. 122.
2. S. XXII. 22. Warren op. cit., p. 160.
3. The above is Conze's summary of the *Sutra* (op. cit., p. 124). See also note on p. 281.
4. Conze, op. cit., p. 122.
5. Ibid., p. 125.
6. Ibid., p. 132.
7. *Buddhist Logic*, Vol. I. p. 113.
8. J. G. Jennings, *The Vedantic Buddhism of the Buddha* (London: OUP, 1947) p. xxxvi.
9. Ibid., pp.xxxvi and xxxviii.
10. Ibid. p. xxxvii.
11. Ibid., pp. 557–61.
12. Ibid., pp. xxxix – xli.
13. Ibid., pp. xli – xliii.
14. Ibid., p. 581 f.
15. Ibid., p. xlix.
16. Ibid., p. xxiii.
17. Ibid., p. xlvii.
18. Ibid., p. xxxvii.
19. *The Philosophy of Anatta: Reconstruction of the Real Teaching of Gotama.* (a Sri Lanka Rationalist Association, Publication, published by Deepanee Printers, H. L. Road, Gangodawila Nugegoda, 1974) p. 58.
20. *Hinduism and Buddhism* (New York: The Wisdom Library Inc.), p. 60.
21. Ibid., p. 62.
22. Ibid., p. 59.
23. Ibid., p. 58.
24. Ibid., p. 76.
25. *Vinaya*, 1.25.
26. W. Rāhula, referring to this story, says: 'Here again it is a simple and natural question, and there is no justification for introducing far-fetched ideas of a metaphysical *Ātman* or Self into the business. They answered that it was better for them to search after themselves. The Buddha then asked them to sit down and explained the *Dhamma* to them. In the available account, in the original text of what he preached to them, not a word is mentioned about an Ātman. (*What the Buddha Taught*, op. cit., p. 62.)
27. For instance W. S. Urquhart says: 'There is a good deal in favour of the view that Buddha, without explicitly stating his position, implicitly admitted an ultimate Reality. The difficulty of distinguishing between pure Being and pure Non-Being is one not easy to say dogmatically, that a teacher who asserts pure Non-Being is not at the same time affirming his belief in an absolute but indescribable Reality.' (*The Vedanta and Modern Thought*, p. 94.)
28. Thus for instance he says: 'These "five Groups" include all the bodily and mental parts and powers of man, and neither any one group, nor any one division of any group is permanent; they are constantly changing, are never for two consecutive moments the same; their nature is to arise and pass away.' (Rhys Davids, T. W. 'On Nirvāna, and on the Buddhist Doctrines of the

"Groups", the Sankhāras, Karma and the "Paths" ', *The Contemporary Review*, XXIX (1877) p. 253.

29. *Wayfarer's Words* (London: Luzac, 1941) Vol. II. pp. 643–4.
30. Ibid., pp. 653–4.
31. Ibid., pp. 656–7.
32. *Studies in the Middle Way* (London: Allen & Unwin), p. 42.
33. Ibid., p. 46. See also *Buddhism* (Harmondsworth: Penguin, 1951) p. 86.
34. Ibid., p. 42.
35. Ibid., p. 42–3.
36. *Buddhism*, p. 86, 87.
37. Ibid., p. 88.
38. Ibid., p. 88.
39. See article '*Soul or no Soul*' in *Ceylon Daily News Vesak Annual*, 1961, p. 13. In this article Humphreys, referring to the radical Theravāda no-soul theory, says: 'I confess that after thirty-five years' work in the Buddhist field, I have never found a Buddhist who behaved as if he or she believed it to be true. . . it is surely a dreary, joyless and unprofitable doctrine. . . . It is worthy of note that no Mahāyānist, of any of the schools, accepts the monk-made teaching of the Theravāda school upon this point.' (pp. 13 and 14).
40. Ibid.
41. See article 'The Self which is not and the self which is' in *World Buddhism*, 1968, p. 18. Also see p. 14 of article referred to in note 39 above.

7 *Self-identity and Nibbāna*

1. Zan Aung, S., *Compendium of Philosophy*, op. cit., p. iv.14.
2. S. iv.19.
3. A. 1.236.
4. *Theragāthā*, 415.
5. Ibid., 1060. Note the word *nibbuto* used here.
6. D. ii.157.
7. The above are quoted by W. Rāhula, *What the Buddha Taught*, op. cit., pp. 36–7.
8. M. iii.264–6. S.B.B. Vol. VI. pp. 305–7.
9. S. I. 38.
10. *Dhammapada*, Nos 96, 98, 99, 197, 198, 199, 200.
11. *Suttanipāta*, 1075.
12. S.B.B. Vol. II. p. 54.
13. M. 1.487 f.
14. Vis: XVI.
15. *Buddhist Essays* (London: Macmillan, 1908) p. 48.
16. *Buddha, His Life and Doctrine*, trans. William Hoey (London: Luzac, 1928), pp. 272–3. About Oldenberg's interpretation of the meaning of Nirvāna there is some dispute. While E. J. Thomas thinks Oldenberg came to the conclusion that *Nirvāna* means annihilation (*History of Buddhist Thought*, p. 127), G. R. Welbon thinks that Thomas has misrepresented Oldenberg, 'who does not dogmatically affirm in any of his writings that *Nirvāna* is annihilation' (*The Buddhist Nirvāna and Its Western Interpreters*, pp. 197 ff).
17. Quoted by Rādhakrishnan, *Indian Philosophy* (London: Allen & Unwin, 1923), p. 449.

18. Quoted by W. D. Guneratna in *World Buddhism* (Vesak Annual, 1969) p. 17.
19. P.T.S. Dictionary, p.362.
20. Ibid., p. 363.
21. Ibid., p. 302.
22. *Milinda's Questions* tr. I. B. Horner (London: Luzac, 1964) Vol. II. pp. 98, 175, 214.
23. Ibid., pp. 87 ff; 195 ff.
24. *Dīgha*, No. 13. S.B.B. Vol. II. p. 300.
25. *Buddha the Humanist* (Decca, Lahore: Paramount Publishers, 1969) pp. 149.
26. Ibid., p.153.
27. *The Psychology of Nirvāna* (London: Allen & Unwin, 1963) p. 30.
28. Ibid., p. 61.
29. Ibid., p. 11.
30. *The Buddhist Nirvāna and Its Western Interpreters* (Chicago and London: The University of Chicago Press, 1968) p. 299.
31. Ibid., p. 302.
32. *Tilakkhaṇa* means three marks or characteristics of existence. They are *anicca*, *dukkha* and *anattā*. These three terms indicate the fundamental 'marks' or 'characteristics' of all existence in the space-time order of reality. They are the hallmarks of existence which point to the fact that all existence in its absolute entirety is but a flux-in-process (*anicca*), having nothing permanent or enduring in the process of change (anattā), and hence inherently incapable of producing any lasting satisfaction (*dukkha*). More simply *anicca* means impermanence, *anattā* means soullessness and *dukkha* means all aspects of suffering. *Anicca* affirms that all conditioned things are impermanent and constantly change; *Anattā* affirms that there is no permanent entity or immortal soul that does not change; *dukkha* affirms that conditioned nature, being what it is, is unsatisfactory, ill, painful and the source of conflict and anxiety. *Dukkha* is a word that has varied shades of meaning and defies precise definition. Perhaps existential anxiety covers much of what *dukkha* means. In my opinion in the *Tilakkhaṇa* analytic we have a comprehensive analysis of the human predicament, in which the anthropological, empirical and experiential problems converge, embracing the whole breadth of human existence.

8 The Biblical View of Man

1. *The Vitality of the Individual in the Thought of Ancient Israel* (Cardiff: University of Wales Press, 1964) pp. 1–2. After a careful investigation of this question, Johnson comes to the conclusion that 'in Israelite thought man is conceived, not so much as in dual fashion as 'Body' and 'Soul', but synthetically as a unit of vital power or (in current terminology) a psycho-physical organism. That is to say, the various members and secretions of the body, such as the bones, the heart, the bowels, and the kidneys, as well as the flesh and the blood, can call be thought of as revealing psychical properties.' (p. 87).
2. *Church Dogmatics* (Edinburgh: T. & T. Clark, 1961) Vol. III, Part 2, p. 382.
3. *Systematic Theology* (London: Nisbet, 1964), Vol. III, p. 437.
4. Genesis 1:27.
5. See *The Interpreter's Bible*, (Nashville, Tenn.: Abingdon Press, 1952) Vol. I. pp. 465–7.

6. *Dogmatics in Outline* (London: S.C.M. Press, 1949) p. 55.

7. *Principles of Christian Theology* (London: S.C.M. Press, 1966) p. 198.

8. *The Bible Doctrine of the Hereafter* (London: Epworth Press, 1958) p. 198.

9. *Religious Ideas of the Old Testament* (London: Epworth Press, 1947) p. 83. W. D. Stacey also makes the same point when he says: 'The Hebrew regarded the soul as almost physical and the physical parts as having psychical functions, so that, whatever activity a man was engaged in, the predominant aspect, be it soul, heart, face, or hand, represented the whole person and included the other parts' (*The Pauline View of Man*, London: Macmillan, 1956, p. 85.)

10. *Heart and Soul and Spirit*, in the 'Preachers' Quarterly,' Vol. III (1957) p. 21. It must be noted that the word *ādām* designates man as a concretely existing group and not in the sense of man as a logical abstraction belonging to a species. It is also important to note that the word *ādām* is derived from *adāmāh* meaning soil or clay. The implication is clear.

11. Genesis 35:18.

12. Job 14:22; Ecclesiastes 12:7.

13. *The Christian Doctrine of Man*, p. 18.

14. *Old Testament Apocalyptic*, p. 28, (Quoted in *Expository Times*, February 1961) p. 132.

15. Wisdom of Solomon 3:1–5; see also 16:14. (N.E.B.)

16. Op. cit., pp. 94 and 95.

17. Matthew 6:25; Mark 8:35; Matthew 2:20 John 10:11.

18. 1 Corinthians 14:7.

19. 1 Corinthians 15:54; (cf. Romans 16:4; Philippians 2:30; 1 Thessalonians 2:8; 2 Corinthians 1:23).

20. Matthew 26:38; Luke 1:46; John. 12:27.

21. Luke 12:19.

22. 2 Corinthians 1:23; 1 Thessalonians 2:8; Ephesians 6:6; Colossians 3:23; Philippians 1:27.

23. Acts 4:32; Philippians 1:27; cf. 2 Kings 9:15.

24. Romans 2:9; 13:1; 2 Corinthians 12:15.

25. Romans 12:5; Ephesians 1:23; cf. Matthew 27:58–59.

26. 1 Corinthians 2:14–15; 15:42–50.

27. Hebrews 6:19; 13; 1 Peter 1:22. 2:11, 25.

28. Hebrews 10:39; James 1:21; 1 Peter 1:9.

29. Ludemann observes that, 'The word *psychē* always appears . . . in connexion which shows the human being in a situation of inferiority, and is not to be brought into agreement with the all-embracing and loftier idea of *psychē* found elsewhere in the classical and Hellenistic usage.' (*Die Anthropologie des Apostels Paulus*, 6. – Quoted by Stacey op. cit. p. 125).

30. Cf. Matthew 6:25; Mark 8:36.

31. *Immortality of the Soul and Resurrection of the Dead*, (New York: The Macmillan Company, 1958), p. 36–7.

32. *Hastings Dictionary of the Bible* (second edition, Edinburgh: T. & T. Clark, 1963) p. 932.

33. 'The psychology of Our Lord's words offers no apparent change from that of the Old Testament. It is popular and primitive, and must not be judged from a scientific or philosophical point of view; but it has one characteristic of great importance. It presents a clear conception of the unity of human nature. There

is no dualism.' (A. C. Headlam, *The Life and Teaching of Jesus the Christ*, p.120.) See also H. W. Robinson, *The Christian Doctrine of Man*, pp. 77f.

34. Op. cit., p. 123. H. W. Robinson points to an Old Testament parallel: 'This is not a systematic dissection of the distinct elements of personality; its true analogy is such an Old Testament sentence as Deut: 6:5, where somewhat similar enumeration emphasizes the totality of the personality.' (*The Christian Doctrine of Man*, p. 108.) Moreover he says: 'The enumeration is not systematic, but hortatory, to emphasize the completeness of the preservation; it should be compared with the somewhat similar enumeration of Deut: 6:5: "Thou shalt love the Lord thy God with all thy heart, and with all thy soul and with all thy might." '(*Mansfield College Essays*, p. 280.)

35. W. Barclay, *The Daily Study Bible, The Revelation of John*, (Edinburgh: The Saint Andrews Press, 1957) Vol. II. p. 13.

36. Having made a comprehensive survey of the New Testament materials on the subject, D. G. R. Owen concludes with the following comment: 'There is little trace of body-soul dualism, instead, man is regarded as a unity. The personal unity that is man can be called, as a whole, either *soma* (body) or *psyche* (soul) or *sarx* (flesh) or *pneuma* (spirit), depending on the point of view from which man is being considered, but the point is that none of these terms refers to a part of man; they all refer to the whole. (*Body and Soul*, p. 196). It must be stressed that there is a homogenous concept of man in the whole of the New Testament underlying differences in detail. W. G. Kummel says: 'Our examination of the view of man in Jesus, Paul and John has shown us that, in spite of differences in terminology and a certain variety in their individual emphasis, all three central forms of the New Testament proclamation pre-suppose essentially the same conception of man,' and with reference to the other writings of the New Testament he says: 'In spite of the fact that we must conclude on exegetical grounds that the two texts Acts 17:28 and 2 Peter 1:4 appear as within the New Testament picture of man, and are to be attributed to the strange intrusion of Hellenistic ideas, yet the rest of the New Testament presents us with a unified picture.' (*Man in the New Testament*, pp. 83 and 95 respectively.)

37. See *In the End God* (London: James Clark & Co., 1950) p. 84.

38. Genesis 2:7.

39. Genesis 3:19.

40. Isaiah 40:6.

41. Psalm 49:12, 20.

42. Psalms 39:5-6.

43. James 4:14.

44. Cf. the Buddhist comparison of the five aggregates to a drop of froth, bubble of water, a mirage, a plantain trunk and to an illusion. (See p. 100.)

45. See Dh. P. 160, 165.

46. *Religion and Christian Faith* (London: Lutterworth Press, 1956) p. 249.

47. *Sin and Salvation* (Madras: C.L.S 1957) pp. 61 f.

48. *Nature and Destiny of Man* (London: Nisbet, 1943) Vol. I. p. 162.

49. *The Distinctive Ideas of the Old Testament* (London: Epworth Press, 1947) p. 150.

50. Psalm 104:29-30.

51. Wisdom of Solomon 2:23-24.

52. *The Pauline View of Man, in relation to its Judaic and Hellenistic Background*, (London: Macmillan, 1956) pp. 128-9.

53. Op. cit., pp. 132–3 (capitals mine).
54. 'From 1 Cor. 5:5 might be deduced a doctrine of the immortality of the spirit, were it not that 1 Thess. 5:23 offers a similar prayer that spirit, soul and body might be preserved at the Parousia. If there is any immortality of the spirit in Paul, it is immortality of the regenerated spirit of the believer. The spirit is in Christ, and has therefore gone beyond death. In time it will be linked with a body more akin to its nature, and its resurrection life will have begun. This is not immortality in anything like the Orphic form. It merely means that the Spirit of God pushes its way through the barrier of death, and recreates for eternity the believer's spirit, before his body dies, and before a resurrection body is possible for him. The natural spirit has no immortality. It has no divine power, it is morally indifferent, it is liable to corruption.' (Op. cit., p. 142.)
55. 1 Corinthians 14:7.
56. 1 Corinthians 15:45.
57. Romans 8:5–8.
58. Isaiah 26:9; Luke 1:46–47; Philippians 1:27.
59. 2 Corinthians 3:18.

9 Man as 'Spirit' – Pneuma

1. Paul Tillich, *Systematic Theology*, op. cit.,Vol. III, p. 23.
2. See *Milinda's Questions*, tr. I. B. Horner (London: Luzac, 1963) Vol. I, pp. 54–6.
3. Colossians 1:16.
4. Colossians 1:17.
5. O. C. Quick, *Doctrines of the Creed* (London: Nisbet; New York: Scribner, 1938) p. 275.
6. Søren Kierkegaard, *Fear and Trembling, Sickness unto Death*, tr. Walter Lowrie (New York: Doubleday, 1954) pp. 146 f.
7. Ibid.
8. 1 Corinthians 12:13; cf. Ephesians 4:4.
9. Ephesians 4:3.
10. Ephesians 4:4.
11. John Macmurray, *Persons in Relation* (London: Faber, 1961) p. 17.
12. 'Even the birds', says Macmurray, 'are not helpless in this sense. The chicks of those species which nest at a distance from their food supply, must be fed by their parents till they are able to fly. But they peck their way out of the egg and a lapwing chick engaged in breaking out of the shell will respond to its mother's danger call by stopping its activity and remaining quite still.' (Ibid., p. 47.)
13. Ibid., pp. 48, 50, and 51.
14. *Interpreting the Universe* (London: Faber, 1933) p. 137.
15. John 15:26.
16. Op. cit., Vol. III, p. 119.
17. John Macquarrie, *Paths in Spirituality* (London: S.C.M. Press, 1972) p. 45.
18. Op. cit., Vol. I. pp. 176–7.
19. Martin Buber, *Between Man and Man*, tr. R. G. Smith (London: Kegan Paul, 1947) p. 144. Buber, born and bred a Jew, has had a great influence on Christian thought, as well as in many other spheres including that of philosophy, psychology and education.

20. William Ernest Hocking, *The Meaning of God in Human Experience* (New Haven and London: Yale University Press, 1963) p. 299.
21. Martin Buber, *I and Thou*, tr. R. G. Smith (Edinburgh: T. & T. Clark, 1937) p. 18.
22. Martin Heidegger, *Being and Time*, tr. John Macquarrie and Edward Robinson (New York: Harper and Row, 1962) p. 117.
23. Quoted by John Baillie, *Our Knowledge of God* (London: OUP, 1939) p. 299.
24. Op. cit., p. 18.
25. Kenneth Cragg, *Christianity in World Perspective* (London: Lutterworth Press, 1969) p. 150.
26. *Conversations*, Graymoor Ecumenical Institute, Sept 1969, p. 3.
27. *Church Dogmatics*, Vol. III, Part 2 (Edinburgh: T. & T. Clark, 1960) p. 354.
28. Ibid., p. 366.
29. Job 34. 14–15; Genesis 6.17; 7.15, 22.
30–32 Op. cit., p. 363.
33. Op. cit., p. 356.
34. Op. cit., p. 360.

10 The Spiritual Body

1. There are only four references to immortality in the New Testament viz: Rom. 2:7; 1 Cor. 15:53–54; 1 Tim. 6:16; 2 Tim. 1:10.
2. 'In the letters, *sōma* has at least five senses that melt into one another in a disconcerting way. There is the body as flesh, the body as the whole man, the body as the principle of redeemable humanity, the body as the means of resurrection, and the Body of Christ, meaning the Church. We are clearly dealing with an inventive and unscientific mind.' (W. D. Stacey, op. cit., p. 182).
3. 'Of all the words which *sōma* translates in the LXX, *bāsār* is the only one which is also used with doctrinal significance, and it is natural to suppose that the primary use in Paul is that which has this parallel in the Old Testament. The other unparalleled uses are those which he developed himself.' (W. D. Stacey, op. cit., p. 182).
4. *The Body–A Study in Pauline Theology* (London: S.C.M. Press, 1947) pp. 13 and 15. My exposition of the word *bāsār* and *sōma* are largely based on this book, which is considered to be an authoritative work. W. D. Stacey commenting on this book says: 'J. A. T. Robinson's study is original and important. He has discovered significance in a neglected term' (op. cit., p. 182. n. 1). Stacey finds that Robinson is a more reliable guide than O. Pfleiderer, who has gone wrong in his interpretation of *Sarx* dichotomously (p. 185), and R. C. Charles, H. W. Robinson and James Moffatt, who do not represent the Pauline view (which J. A. T. Robinson does), when they say that the destruction of the old body must precede the creation of the new (p. 187). C. H. Dodd's contention that 'the body is the individual self as an organism' needs modification, says Stacey, in the light of J. A. T. Robinson's contention that 'individuality is not the key to the meaning of *sōma*' (p. 191). Stacey claims that Robinson's 'great contribution is the discovery that the various 'bodies' of Paul are communal conceptions. . . . Robinson has done us the service of demonstrating the quality of the word *sōma* in its highest use, and of showing that, in true Hebrew

fashion, there is a sense of corporateness behind every use of *sōma* in Paul.'
(p. 188.)

5. Ibid., p. 31.
6. 1 Corinthians 1:29.
7. *Immortality of the Soul and Resurrection of the Dead* (London: Epworth Press, 1964) p. 26.
8. *In the End, God* (London: James Clark & Co., 1950) p. 85.
9. J. A. T. Robinson, *The Body* (London: S.C.M. Press, 1947) p. 31. 'Although the flesh is by nature mortal,' says W. D. Stacey, 'the body is mortal only in one sense and under certain conditions. There is a *sōma* of the resurrection. We must examine *sōma* in its own right, apart from its similarities with *sarx*. In the first place, the *sōma* is not merely capable of redemption, but is the precise term Paul uses when he wants to speak of human life dedicated to God. In Rom. 8: 1-11, both the flesh and the body, under the dominion of sin, are dead, but v. 11 reveals that the body does not die inevitably, but may be raised up by the Spirit. The purpose of the body is not fornication (1 Cor. 6:13), which is a sin against it (v. 18), but the glorification of God (v. 20). The body can be dedicated (Rom 12:1) and the rest of the chapter shows that this means the whole man, physical, mental and emotional, not merely man in his physical strength.' (Op. cit., p. 186.)
10. Ibid., p. 31 note 1.
11. Ibid., p. 32.
12. Op. cit., p. 27.
13. J. A. T. Robinson draws attention to this point in *In the End, God*, pp. 87 f.
14. *Nature and Destiny of Man* (London: Nisbet, 1943) Vol. II, pp. 305 and 307.
15. Ibid., 6:15.
16. *Theological Word Book of the Bible*, ed. Alan Richardson (London: S.C.M. Press, 1960) p. 35.
17. 1 Corinthians 6:19.
18. Ibid., 6:15.
19. 2 Corinthians 4:10; and Philippians 1:20.
20. Romans 12:1.
21. St Paul seems to elaborate the idea in terms of St John 12:24, viz: 'Truly I say to you, unless a grain of wheat falls into the earth and dies, it remains alone, but if it dies it bears much fruit.' Strictly speaking the seed does not die, because the power of germination remains. But the Apostle was not thinking in terms of a strictly natural process. He did not mean that there was a power of germination in the dead body which naturally grew into another body. Belief in natural survival amounts to belief in the immortality of the Soul which the Apostle rejected. The analogy of the seed must not be pressed too far. A similar analogy – the simile of the mango stone – is found in the *Milindapañha*, 71 (*Milinda's Questions*) tr. I. B. Horner (London: Luzac, 1963) Vol. I, p. 106.
22. *The Christian Doctrine of the Church, Faith and the Consummation*, Dogmatics Vol. III. tr. Olive Wyon (London: Lutterworth, 1962) p. 413.
23. 'The Christian doctrine of eternal life', says William Temple, 'is not a mere proclamation of survival; it is a call to life in fellowship with God, and in Him with our fellows, begun here and perfected hereafter. Its characteristic expression is not the immortality of the soul, but the resurrection of the body. Of course this does not mean the revivification of the material particles ('flesh

and blood cannot inherit the Kingdom of God'), but the restoration of the whole personal being in complete continuity with the life on earth, in a fuller and richer mode of expression than is possible here and now. We have in this the confident hope that every grace of character in those whom we have loved and lost is still theirs in even fuller measure than during their days on earth.' (*The Christian Hope of Eternal Life*, S.P.C.K., p. 7. Quoted by E. A. Baker, *William Temple and His Message* (London: Penguin Books, 1946 p. 104.)

24. Paul Tillich, *Systematic Theology* (London: Nisbet, 1964) Vol. III, p. 440.

25. See Miguel de Unamuno, *The Tragic Sense of Life*, tr. J. E. C. Flitch (New York: Dover, 1954; and London: Fontana, 1962); Charles Hartshorne's essay on 'Time, Death and Eternal Life' in *The Logic of Perfection* (Lasalle, Ill., 1962); Wolfhart Pannenberg, *What is Man* (Philadelphia: Fortress Press, 1970); David Edwards; *The Last Things Now* (London: S.C.M. Press, 1969).

26. John Hick, *Death and Eternal Life* (London: Collins; and New York: Harper & Row, 1976). See pp. 213–26.

27. Ibid., p. 220.

28. Ibid., p. 279.

29. Ibid., p. 282.

30. Ibid.

31. Ibid.

11 Progressive Sanctification

1. Quoted by Nārada Thera in *The Buddha and His Teaching*, op. cit., p. 485.

2. *Truth and Revelation* (London: Geoffrey Bles, 1953) p. 137.

3. *The Destiny of Man* (London: Geoffrey Bles 1937) p. 279.

4. *Systematic Theology*, op. cit., Vol: III, p. 444.

5. *Nature, Man and God* (London: Macmillan, 1960) p. 464.

6. *Expository Times* (Edinburgh: T & T Clark, 1965), p. 464.

7. John Hick, *Evil and the God of Love* (London: Macmillan, 1966) p. 383.

8. Ibid., pp. 382–3.

9. *Principles of Christian Theology* (London: S.C.M. Press,1966) p. 328.

10. *The Last Things*, p. 46, quoted by Macquarrie, ibid., p. 329.

11. In this context we could probably understand rebirth as a symbol, as Tillich and others have suggested, which points to the higher or lower forces (*kusala* and *akusala karma*) present in every person, and which fight with each other on higher or lower levels in the fulfilment of one's destiny. It is a continuous process of death to self so that new life may arise. In this light to be born a rooster would mean that lustful forces will prevail; to be born a swan would mean that aesthetic qualities would prevail. *Karma* would thus symbolise the vices and virtues which will continue until evil is completely purged and the conflict comes to an end. This is an area for profitable dialogue between Buddhists and Christians in the attempt at mutual understanding.

12. *Encyclopaedia of Religion and Ethics* (E.R.E.) Vol. XI, p. 837. Although the aim of the parable is not to give us details of the life after death but to challenge us with our duty in this life it cannot be denied that the state of the afterlife depicted here is true to what Jesus knew about it.

13. Ibid., p. 837.

14. Luke 3:8.

15. See *Hastings Dictionary of the Bible* (Edinburgh: T. & T. Clark, 2nd edition, 1963) pp. 6–7.

16. E.R.E., p. 837.

17. A. T. Hanson refers to 'other passages in the N.T. where Christ's presence among the dead, or His victory over the realm of the dead, is at least alluded to; compare Matt. 27:52; Luke 23:43; Acts 2:27, 31; Phil. 2:10; 1 Tim. 3:10; Rev. 5:13.' (See article, 'Descent into Hell' in *A Dictionary of Christian Theology*, ed. Alan Richardson, p. 93.

18. Who are 'the spirits in prison?' Charles Bigg says: 'The context seems to imply that they were those of the men who refused to listen to Noah. *Pneumata* may be used of men after death (Heb. xii:23), and the *nekrois* of iv.6 fixes this as the right sense.' (*A Critical and Exegetical Commentary on the Epistles of St. Peter and St. Jude*, International Critical Commentary (Edinburgh: T. & T. Clark, 1920), p. 162). Edward Gordon Selwyn, in *The First Epistle of St. Peter*, (Macmillan, 1946), while acknowledging that the above view has weighty support (p. 316) says: ' . . . the linguistic and grammatical considerations are in favour of the phrase "the spirits in prison" referring to those archetypal spirits of evil whose rebellion led to the wickedness which brought about the Flood, and whose Fall was regarded by one tradition of Jewish teaching as the *fons et origo* of human sin (p. 353). Nevertheless, he finds Calvin's view 'of great interest' and quotes his words in a footnote as follows: 'These holy dead of the Jewish faith were said to be "in prison", because they had been "confined" (*constringi*) by the Law during life, and after death *solicito Christi desiderio*. St Peter alludes to the disobedient of Noah's day because at that time the unbelievers greatly outnumbered the believers. From the triumph of the grace of God in that case, therefore, the Christians of later days should take heart, when they found themselves so small a minority in an unbelieving world.' (p. 317.) According to Albert E. Barnett, 'The simplest meaning is that our Lord descended between His passion and resurrection, to preach to certain spirits imprisoned in Hades (Hades, or Sheol, was no longer regarded as the abode of pitiless shades, but partly as a place of punishment and partly as an intermediate state). (*The Interpreters Bible* New York: Abingdon Press Nashville 1957), Vol: xii. p. 132).

19. On this verse E. G. Selwyn comments: '"The dead" in iv:6 has been variously interpreted, as connoting (1) all the dead, (2) those who died at the time of the Flood, (3) those who have died in martyrdom, either in St Peter's time or in previous persecutions (4) Christians who have died. The last two of these views are by no means exclusive, the problem of martyrdom being not a different problem from that of the decease of Christians generally, but rather the point at which this general problem became most acute.' (Op. cit., p. 338.) Further he says: 'There are, however, weighty reasons, on grounds both of language and of context, particularly the latter, for believing that "the dead" of 1 Pet. iv.6 are not the dead as a whole (as probably in Jn. v:25, and certainly in Jn. v:28, 29), but only a portion of them relevant to the writer's immediate argument, namely those Christians who had died, often in circumstances of obloquy and persecution, since receiving the Gospel.' (Op. cit., p. 354.)

20. Note the words 'under the earth' which is a reference to *Hades*.

21. Here too Christ's triumph is extended to 'under the earth'. E. G. Selwyn, having traced the idea of Christ's *Descensus ad Infernos* in other writings of the New Testament, particularly Rom. 10:6–8, Eph. 4:8–10, Phil. 2:10 and Rev.

5: 13 comes to the conclusion that: 'The beliefs, then, that our Lord immediately after His death went to the underworld, and that His redemptive work embraced that region as well as earth and heaven, is part of the current coin of N.T. teachings.' (Op. cit., p. 322). He also points out that the belief in Christ's descent into Hades 'is a well attested belief in the Church of the second century' (p. 340), although it is not based on 1 Peter 3:19 and 4:6. The sources of this belief are to be found in other passages quoted in the patristic writings (e.g. Heb. 11:12; Mat. 12:29, 40; 8:11, Lk. 13:28, 29; Eph. 4:9; Col. 2:15 p. 344).

22. Op. cit., p. 287. A. T. Hanson too makes a relevant comment: 'The suggestion found in 1 Peter that the descent gave an opportunity for those who died before Christ to hear the gospel is rather too mythological for modern minds, but it may be regarded as a hopeful symbol of the destiny of those who have died without ever having heard the good news of Christ. Some means must be found for safeguarding the insight that the generations before Christ were not deprived of the gospel.'

23. See also Matthew 5:26; 18:34.

24. According to Buddhism there are a number of hells. In *Anguttara* 1.141 seven tortures are described. 'The king of hell, Yama, hands the culprit over to the keepers of hell, who torment their victims by thrusting an iron stake through each hand and foot, and breast (the 'five-fold' bonds): they chop him with axes; they set him upside down and chop him with adzes; they fix him to the chariot and move it backwards and forwards over the burning ground; they make him go up and down mountains of burning coal; they put him head first into a blazing copper cauldron (*lohakumbhi*); they throw him into the great hell (*Mahāniraya*).'

25. *True Humanism*, tr. M. and R. Adamson (London: Geoffrey Bles, 1938) p. 56.

26. World Council of Churches, Kandy Conference 1967, Document.

27. St. John 3:16. Also St. John 5:24; 6:40; 47; 1 John 5:13; 1 Tim. 1:16.

28. St. John 17:3.

29. See above p. 113.

30. See 2 Corinthians 3:18.

31. *From Glory To Glory: Texts from Gregory of Nyssa's Mystical Writings*, ed. Jean Danielou and Herbert Musurillo (New York: Charles Scribner's Sons, 1961; and London: John Murray, 1962), Sermon 8, pp. 212–13.

32. *Readings in St. John's Gospel* (London: Macmillan, 1963) pp. 218, 219, 220.

12 The Kingdom of God – Community of Love

1. *Systematic Theology*, Vol. III, p. 382.

2. Matthew 16:24–25; Luke 9:22–24.

3. Daily Study Bible, *The Gospel of St. Luke*, —p. 122.

4. Quoted by A. C. Mc Giffert, *A History of Christian Thought*. Vol. II, p. 226. Eckhart is considered to be a pantheist and although his theology cannot help us much in our present investigation, on the level of experience there is much that we can learn from him. In *Mysticism East and West*, Rudolf Otto has pointed out striking similarities as well as differences between Eckhart and Sankara.

5. *Theologia Germanica*, ed. J. Bernhart, p. 157. This treatise has sometimes been

suspected of pantheism, but its doctrine is now generally recognised as perfectly orthodox.

6. Suso, *Büchlein von der Wahrheit*, ch. 4. Quoted by John Hick, *Death and Eternal Life*, op. cit., p. 445.

7. *Mysticism*, p. 508. Quoted by John Hick, ibid., pp. 445–6.

8. *The Threefold Life of Man*, ch. VI, p. 88. Quoted by John Hick, ibid., pp. 444–5.

9. *Mysticism*, pp. 497–8. Quoted by John Hick, ibid., p. 444.

10. Op. cit., p. 446.

11. *The Phenomenon of Man* (London: Collins, 1959) p. 263.

12. Ibid., p. 262.

13. I have referred to the Hindu ideal because, as we have seen, *Nirvāna* has sometimes been interpreted in terms of absorption into Brahman in which self identity disappears. It is of interest to note how the later Hindu philosophy moved away from the classical non-dualism (*Advaita Vada*) championed by Sankara (eighth century A.D.), who incidentally was called a crypto-Buddhist by an eminent Indian critic, although, in fact, Sankara was one who combated Buddhism. It was Rāmānuja (eleventh century A.D.), as great a thinker as Sankara, who taught a 'modified non-dualism' (*Visista-advaita*) or 'difference-non-difference'. While he accepted the fundamental Vedānta teaching that Brahman and Ātman, God and man, are one, he argued that they are not identical and that there always is a difference which allows for personal devotion. In personal devotion one seeks union with Brahman, but not identity. Madhva (thirteenth century) carried this idea further, claiming that the great phrase *Tat tvam asi* (that thou art) was wrongly interpreted and by an ingenious textual emendation came to the conclusion that it really meant 'thou art not That'. Thus a dualism was reached.

14. Love is not merely an emotion, but a moving dynamic power of life. It is the dynamic self-affirmation of life in spite of that which threatens life and it includes all dimensions of life. Love is one, but it finds expression in a hierarchy of 'qualities'; in *epithumia* – the desire for sensual fulfilment; in *erōs* – the passion for reunion with the good, the true and the beautiful; in *philia* – the drive for mutual relationship between persons; and in *agapē* – the all-embracing and self-transcending quality of love.

15. Op. cit., p. 265–6.

16. M. C. D'Arcy develops this idea in *The Mind and Heart of Love* (New York: Meridian Books 1956) ch. 7.

17. Philippians 2: 7–8 (N.E.B.)

18. Ibid., 2:9–11.

19. The injunction to love one's neighbour as oneself is reiterated in Matt: 19:19; 22:39; Rom: 13:9; Gal: 5:14; James 2:8. This injunction has been variously interpreted, some seeing in it a vindication and some a limitation of self-love.

20. 1 Corinthians 15:54.

21. 1 John 3:14.

22. Romans 8: 38–9.

23. 1 Corinthians 13:8 (R.S.V.).

24. *Preaching the Gospel of the Resurrection* (London: The Bevan Memorial Lecture of Adelaide, Lutterworth Press, 1951) p. 44.

25. *Principles of Christian Theology*, p. 321.

13 Anattā and God

1. *Church Dogmatics*, op. cit., p. 345.
2. Ibid.
3. Ibid., p. 346.
4. Ibid., p. 348–9.
5. *Khuddaka Nikāya*, I. 3:8.
6. *A Buddhist Critique of the Christian Concept of God* (Colombo: Lake House Investments Ltd. 1974) See specially ch. 5, 'God as Experience'.
7. Ibid., p. 10.
8. Ibid., p. 12.
9. Ibid., p. 180. A critique of this book appears in *Dialogue*, Vol. II no. 3 and Vol. III, no. 1, published by the Study Centre for Religion and Society, 490/5, Havelock Road, Colombo 6, Sri Lanka. (Referred to by T. R. V. Murthi, *The Central Philosophy of Buddhism, op. cit.*, p. 235.)
10. Ibid., p. 185.
11. See T. V. R. Murthi, *The Central Philosophy of Buddhism – A Study of the Mādhyamika System* (London: Allen & Unwin, 1955) pp. 229–30.
12. E. R. Sarathchandra, *Buddhist Psychology of Perception* (Ceylon University Press, 1958) p. 101.
13. *Mādhyamika Kārikās of Nāgārjuna*, ed., L. de la V. Poussin xxiv. 10.
14. D. C. Wijewardana, *Revolt in the Temple* (Colombo Sinha Publications, 1953) p. 398.
15. H. Oldenberg, *Buddha: His Life, His Doctrine, His Order* tr. William Hoey from the German (London: Luzac, 1928) p. 283 (italics mine).
16. *Katha upanishad*, I. ii. 18. See also I. iii. 16; II. 1.3. Also see *Bhagavad Gita*, 2:20.
17. *Buddha: His Life, His Teaching, His Order*, tr. William Hoey (London: Luzac, 1928) p. 284.
18. Romans 11:33, 36.
19. Quoted by William Hamilton, 'The New Essence of Christianity' in *Toward a New Christianity: Readings in the Death of God Theology*, ed. Thomas J. J. Altizer (New York: Harcourt Brace and World, 1967) p. 269.
20. Op. cit., p. 41.
21. Ibid., p. 4.
22. Ibid., pp. 43–4.
23. Alfred North Whitehead, *Science and the Modern World* (New York: Macmillan, 1926) p. 275.

14 The Practical Relevance of the Anattā-pneuma Concept

1. Galatians 3:28.
2. Harold K. Schilling, *The New Consciousness in Science and Religion* (London: S.C.M. Press, 1973) p. 25.
3. Ibid., p. 26.
4. See passage quoted by Schilling, op. cit., p. 81.
5. Ibid., p. 82.
6. Quoted in *Christian Faith and the Chinese Revolution* – Workshop Reports from an Ecumenical Colloquium in Louvain, Belgium, September 9–14, 1974. (Mimeograph publication, Lutheran World Federation, Pro Mundi Vita) p. 15.

7. Karl Marx, *Selections in Feuerbach*, p. 244.
8. Martin Buber, *Between Man and Man*, tr. R. G. Smith (London: Kegan Paul, 1947) pp. 147–8.
9. *Das Kapital*, p. 23.
10. See Robert K. Merton, *Social Theory and Social Structure*, and Emile Durkheim, *Le Suicide*.
11. *The Speeches and Writings of Che Guevara*, ed. John Gerassi (London: Weidenfeld & Nicolson, 1968), p. 48.
12. The above four quotations are taken from *Quotations from Chairman Mao Tse-Tung*, with an introduction by A. Doak Barnett (New York: Bantam Books, 1967) pp. 95, 138, 154, 156, respectively.
13. R. R. Karanjia, *The Mind of Mr. Nehru*, (London: Allen & Unwin, 1960) pp. 32–6.
14. Theodore Roszak, *The Making of a Counter Culture* (London: Faber, 1970).
15. John Macquarrie, *God and Secularity* (London: Lutterworth Press, 1968) p. 66.
16. *Jesus Rediscovered* (London: Collins/Fontana Books, 1969) p. 61.
17. St. James 4:1–2.
18. *The Burning Fountain* (Bloomington: Indiana University Press, 1954) ch. 1.
19. See M. M. Thomas, *Man and the Universe of Faiths* (The Christian Literature Society, P.O. Box 501, Madras 600003, 1975) pp. 121 f.

Glossary of Pali and Sanskrit Terms

Abhidhamma	higher Dhamma (Metaphysics)
Abhūtam	unbecome
Ādicca samuppanna	arising without cause
Ajātaṃ	unborn
Ākāso	space
Akatan	unmade
Amata	undying, eternal
Ananta	limitless
Anantara	proximity
Anattā	Doctrine of no-self
Anicca	change, impermanence
Anidassana	non-manifestative
Animittavimokkha	conditionless deliverance
Anupādhiseko	without the conditions of life
Āpo	fluidity
Appamāṇa	immeasurable
Arūpaloka	formless world
Asaṃkhata	unconditioned
Attābhūva	selfhood
Attakilamatānuyoga	self-mortification
Attha (artha)	good, profit
Avigatta	abeyance
Avyākata	undeclared (questions)
Avyāpāda	kindness
Bhārahāram	burden-bearer
Brahmā	creator-God in Hinduism
Brahma Vihāra	sublime states
Brahmacariya	life of chastity, celibacy
Brahman	godhead or the Absolute in Hinduism

Citta	mind
Dharmas	elements
Dhuva	stable
Diṭṭhūpādāna	clinging to views
Dosa	hatred
Dosakkhaya	free from hatred
Dukkha	pain, unsatisfactoriness, existential anxiety
Duggati	lower world
Jāla	net
Jarā	old age
Jāta	birth
Jīva	soul
Kāmaloka	world of sense
Kāmasukhallikānuyoga	self-indulgence
Kamma	action
Kammavega	action forces
Kathāvatthu	an Abhidhamma text
Kevala	absolute
Khandhaparinibbāna	disintegration of the aggregates (or body)
Khemam	security
Kilesaparinibbāna	death of defilements
Kammabhava	pre-natal kamma process
Kusalakamma	good deeds
Lokuttara	supra-mundane
Mahābhūta	great Elements
Manussā	human beings
Manas	mind (mano-Pali)
Moha	delusion
Moksha	salvation
Na jāyate	non born
Na me so attā	this is not my 'self'
Nāma-rūpa	mind-matter (name-form)
Natthi	absence

Nibbāna Nagara	city of Nibbāna
Niraya	hell
Nirvāna	destruction of craving, the ultimate Goal
Nityah	permanent
Paccaya	relation
Pañcakkhandha	five-fold aggregates of personality
Paramasukham	highest bliss
Paramattha	absolute
Parinibbāyi	extinguished
Pariññeyya	comprehend
Paṭisandhi-viññāṇa	rebirth linking consciousness
Paṭhavī	earth
Ponobhavikā	causing rebirth
Pubbekatahetu	caused by previous deeds
Puggala	person
Purānah	primeval
Rāga	lust
Rāgakkhaya	free from lust
Rūpaloka	world of form
Sabbe Saṃkhārā aniccā	all formations are impermanent
Sacchikata	true experience
Samanantara	contiguity
Saṃkhārā	karma-formations
Saṃsāra	wheel of becoming
Saṃsāravisuddhi	deliverence from sansara
Saññā	perception
Santaṃ	peace
Sassatadiṭṭhi	theory of eternalism
Sat-Cit-Ānanda	absolute Being, absolute conscious-ness, absolute Bliss
Satyasamkalpah	real thoughts
Saupādhisesa	with conditions of life
Sivaṃ	happiness
Skandha	aggregate
Sukha	pleasure
Suññatā	emptiness

Taṇhā	craving
Tat twam asi	that thou art
Tejo	fire
Tiracchānayoni	animal realm
Ucchedadiṭṭhi	theory of nihilism
Upādāna	clinging
Upalabhyate	got at
Uppādarūpa	secondary elements
Uppatibhava	pre-natal life process
Vimrāyuh	free from death
Vinipāta	fall (to a lower abode)
Viññāṇa santati	process of consciousness
Vohāra	conventional (vacana-speech)

Index of Names

General Index